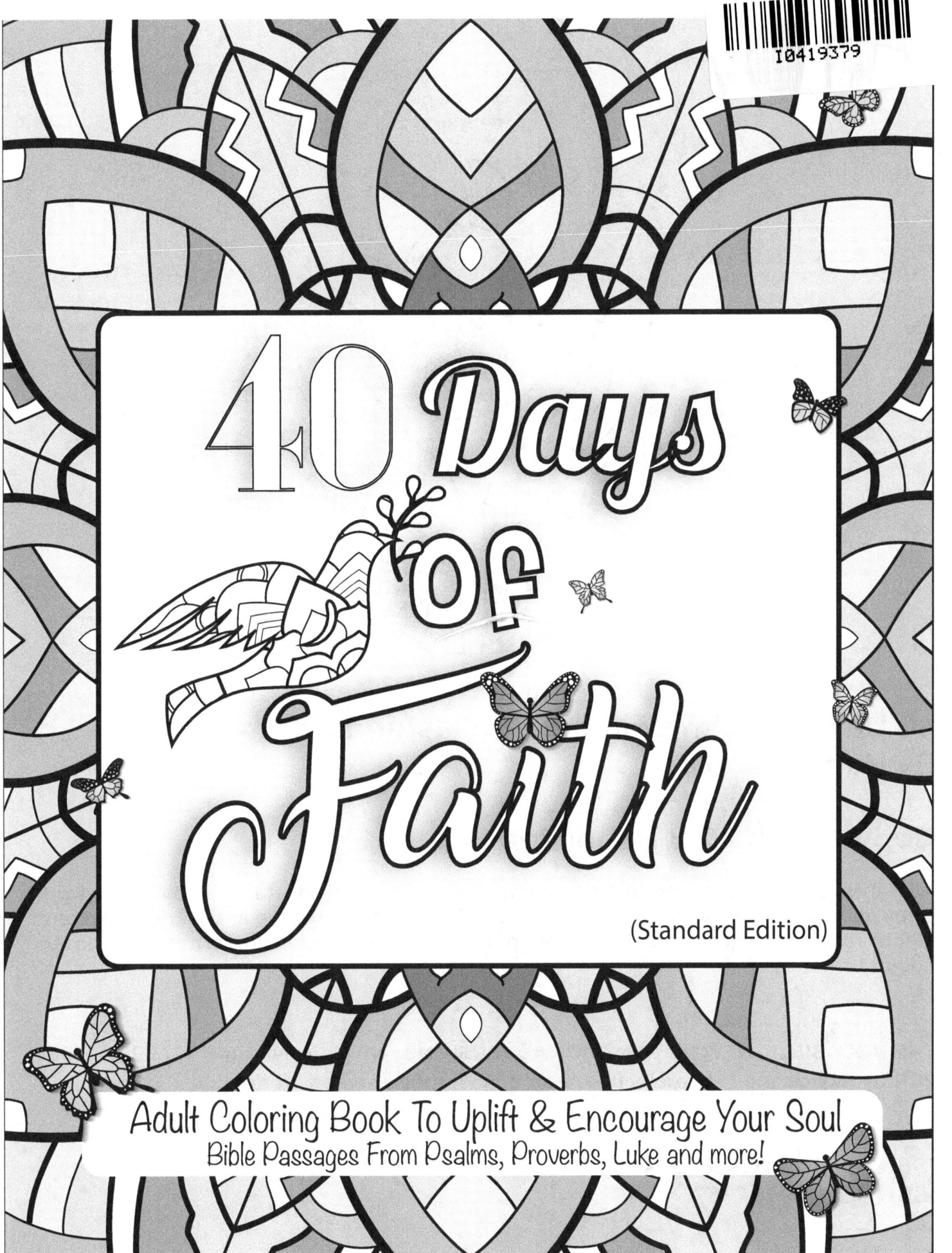

40 Days Of Faith

(Standard Edition)

Adult Coloring Book To Uplift & Encourage Your Soul
Bible Passages From Psalms, Proverbs, Luke and more!

I will strengthen you & help you;
I will uphold you with my
righteous hand.

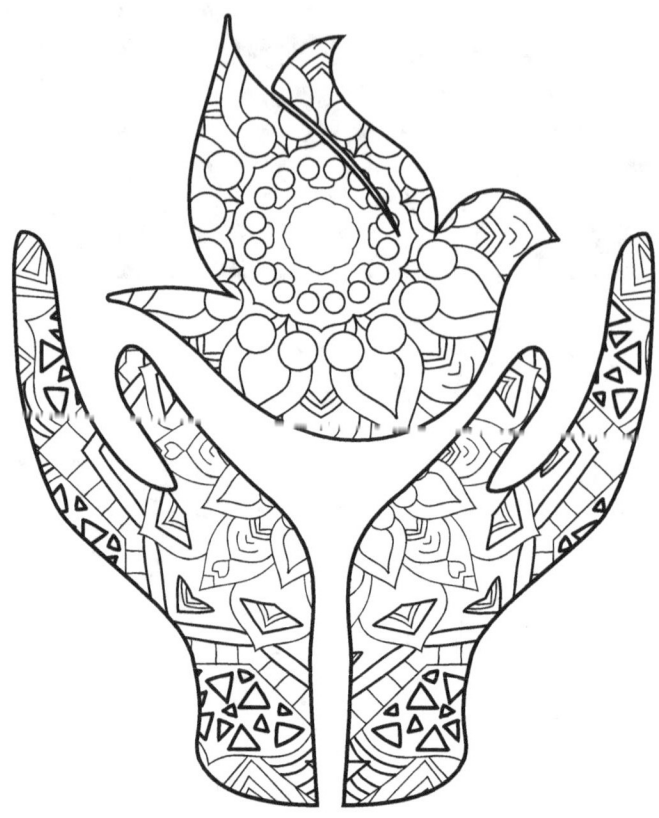

40 Days Of Faith Coloring Book (standard)
By Happi Peoples

Copyright © 2018 Happi Peoples

Scriptures Taken From
THE HOLY BIBLE, NEW INTERNATIONAL VERSION®, NIV® Copyright © 1973, 1978, 1984, 2011 by Biblica, Inc.™ Used by permission. All rights reserved worldwide.

ISBN-13: 978-1719384964
ISBN-10: 1719384967

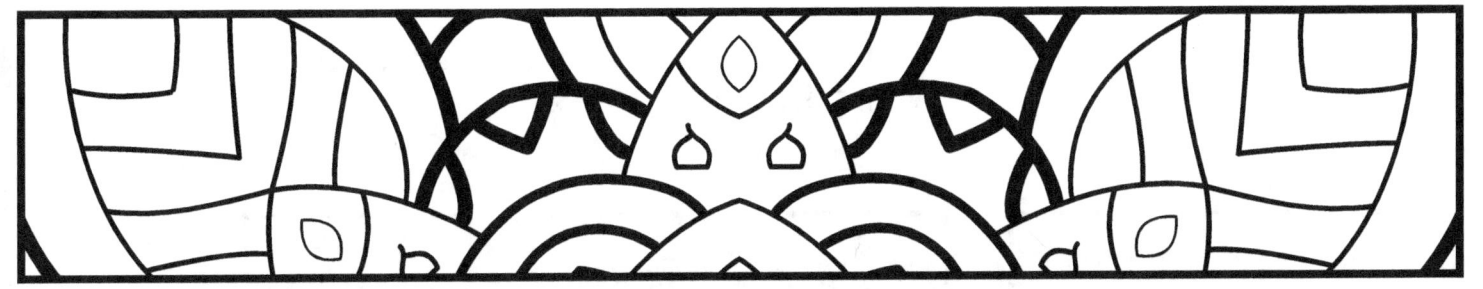

READ THIS, BEFORE YOU COLOR!

SPECIAL BONUS...
This book includes a FREE Download PDF Coloring Book (order online)
Join the mailing list for more goodies, special discounts, and free coloring pages: **www.Wix.com/HappiPeoples**

Email: booksbyhappi@gmail.com

Subject: 40 Days Of Faith Digital (Standard)

Please include your reciept number or amazon order number in the email message. (NO ATTACHMENTS PLEASE)

If you're a fan of Adult Coloring books, I would personally love to hear from you.

Give me a call at **1-844-473-6776** with questions, comments, and feedback about the type of designs you would like to see in my next book.

In the meantime share your coloirng pages with me on...

Instagram:
www.instagram.com/HappiPeoples

Pinterest:
www.pinterest.com/HappiPeoples

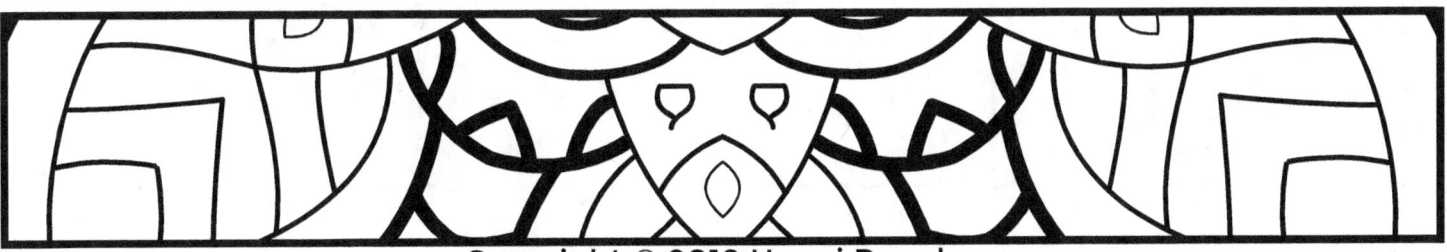

40 Days Of Faith Coloring Book (standard)
Sample Artwork

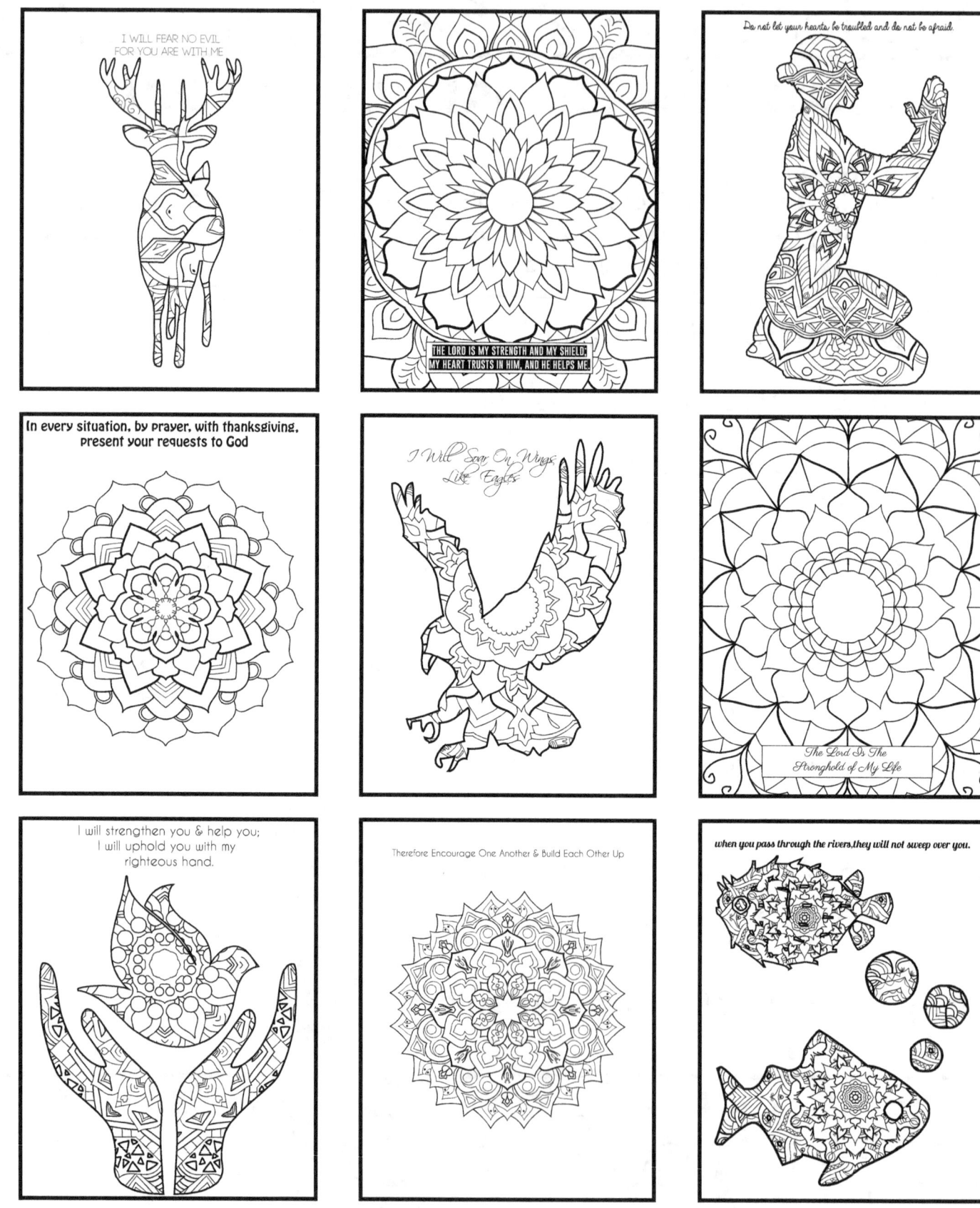

40 Days Of Faith Coloring Book (standard)
Sample Artwork

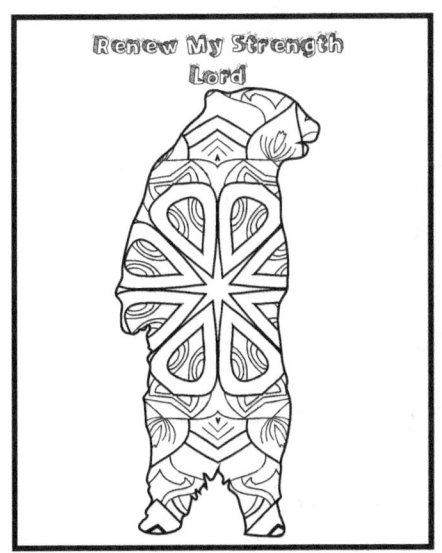

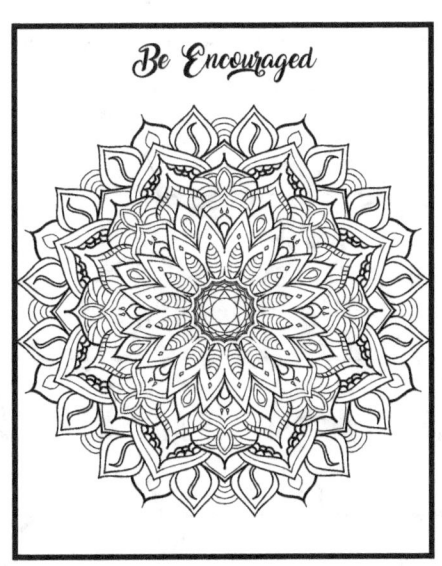

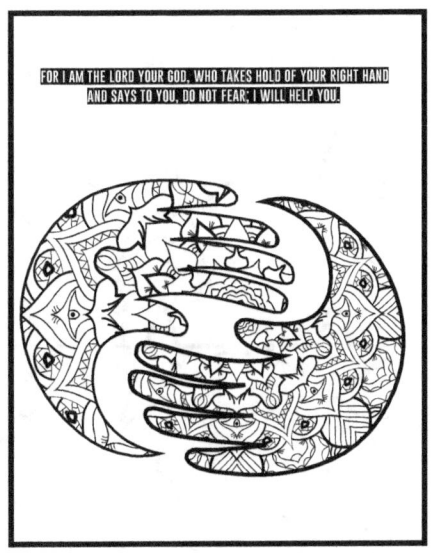

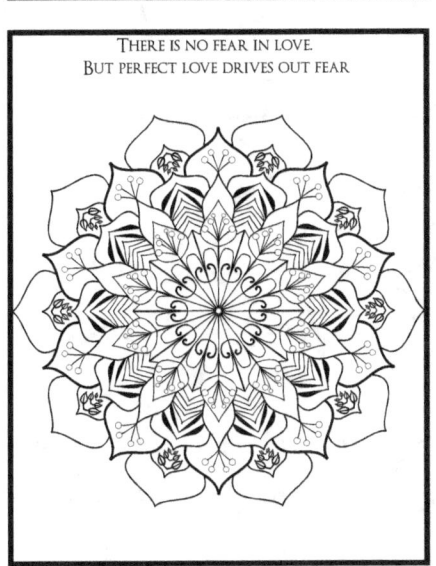

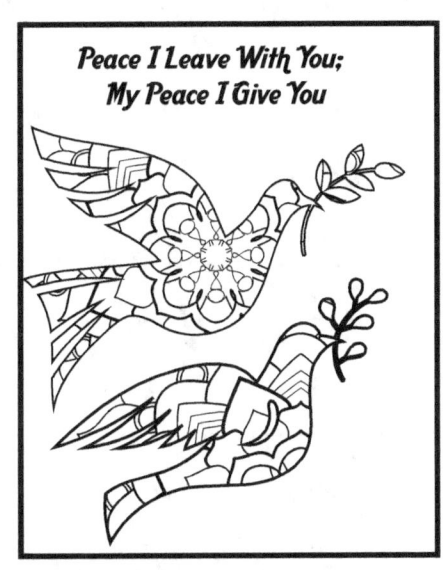

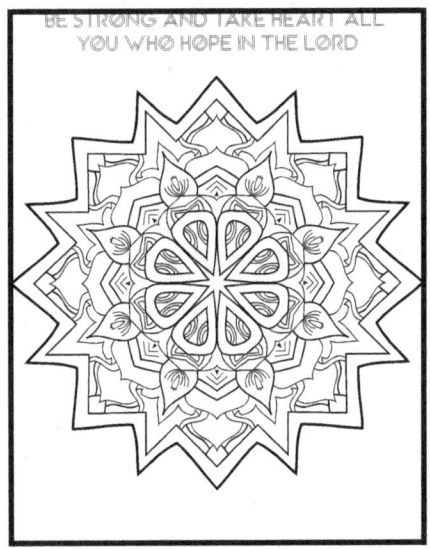

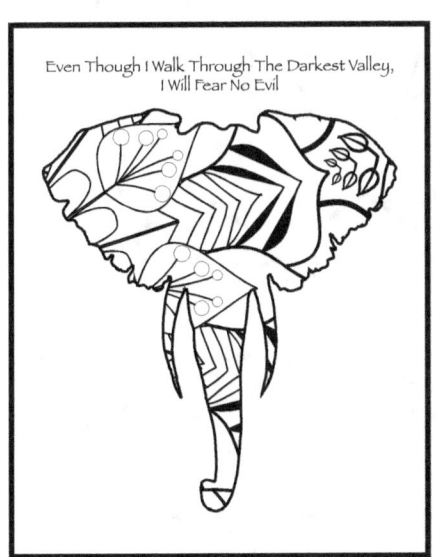

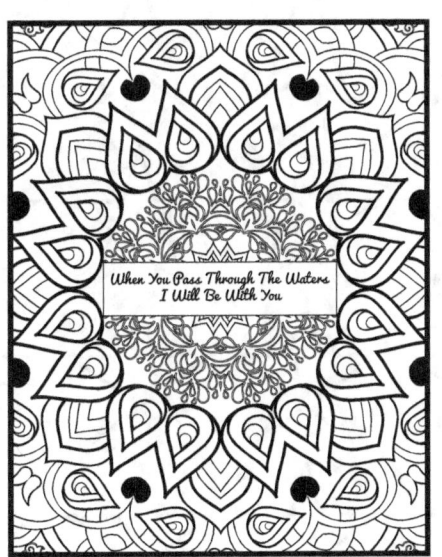

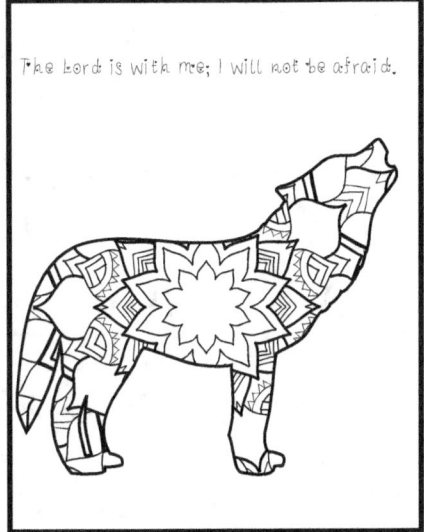

COLOR TEST PAGE

COLOR TEST PAGE

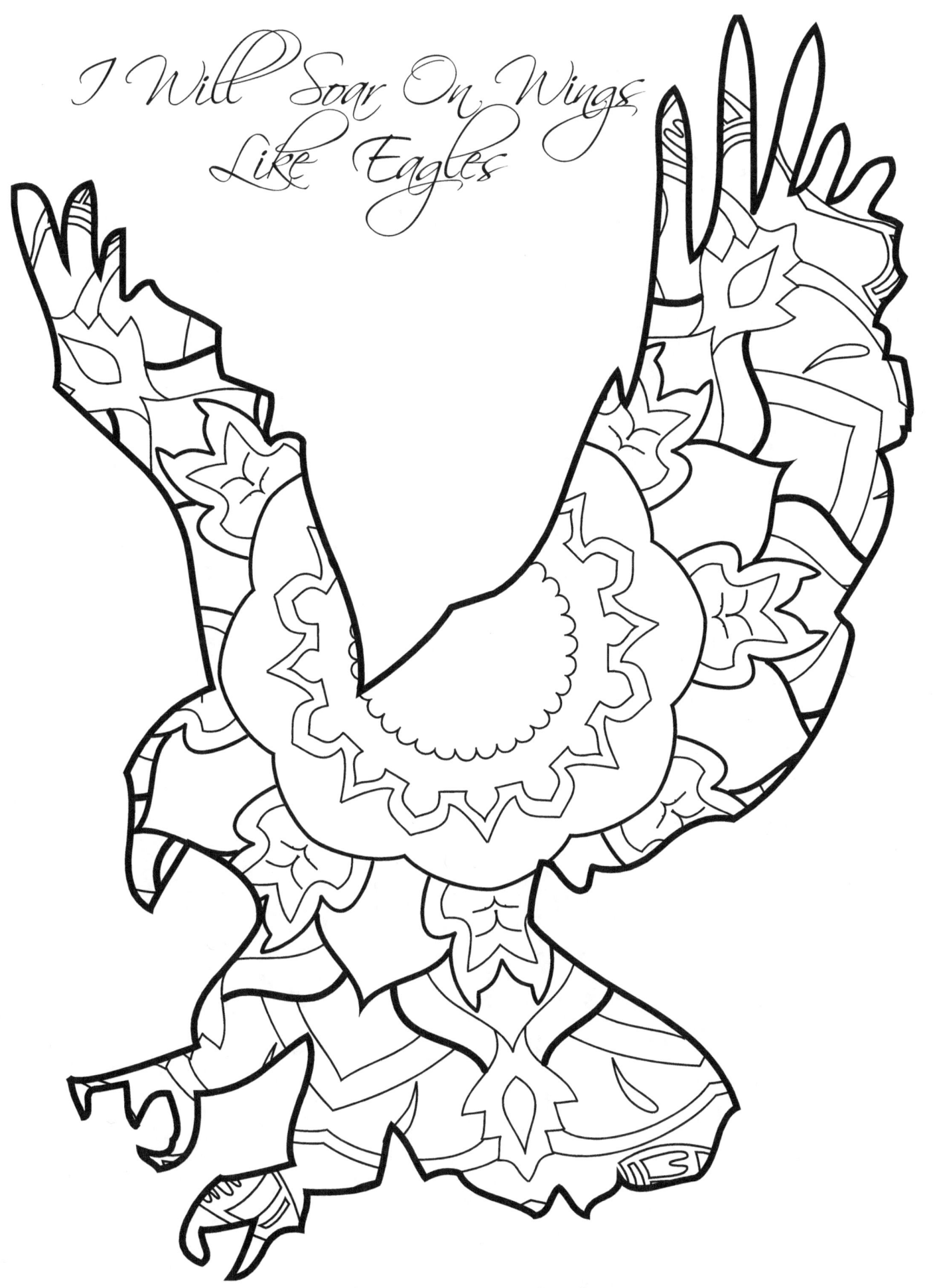

I Will Soar On Wings Like Eagles

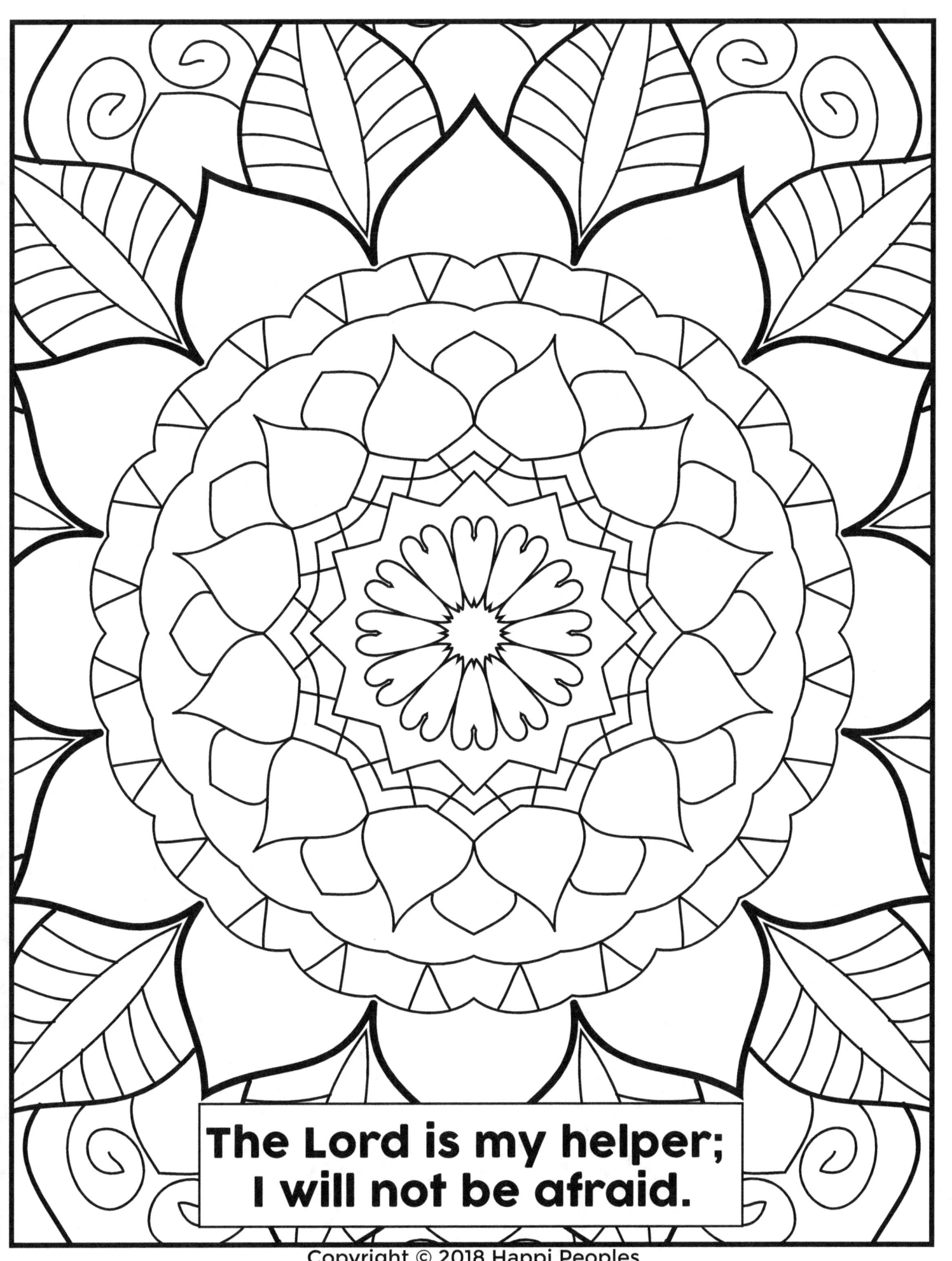

The Lord is my helper;
I will not be afraid.

Therefore Encourage One Another & Build Each Other Up

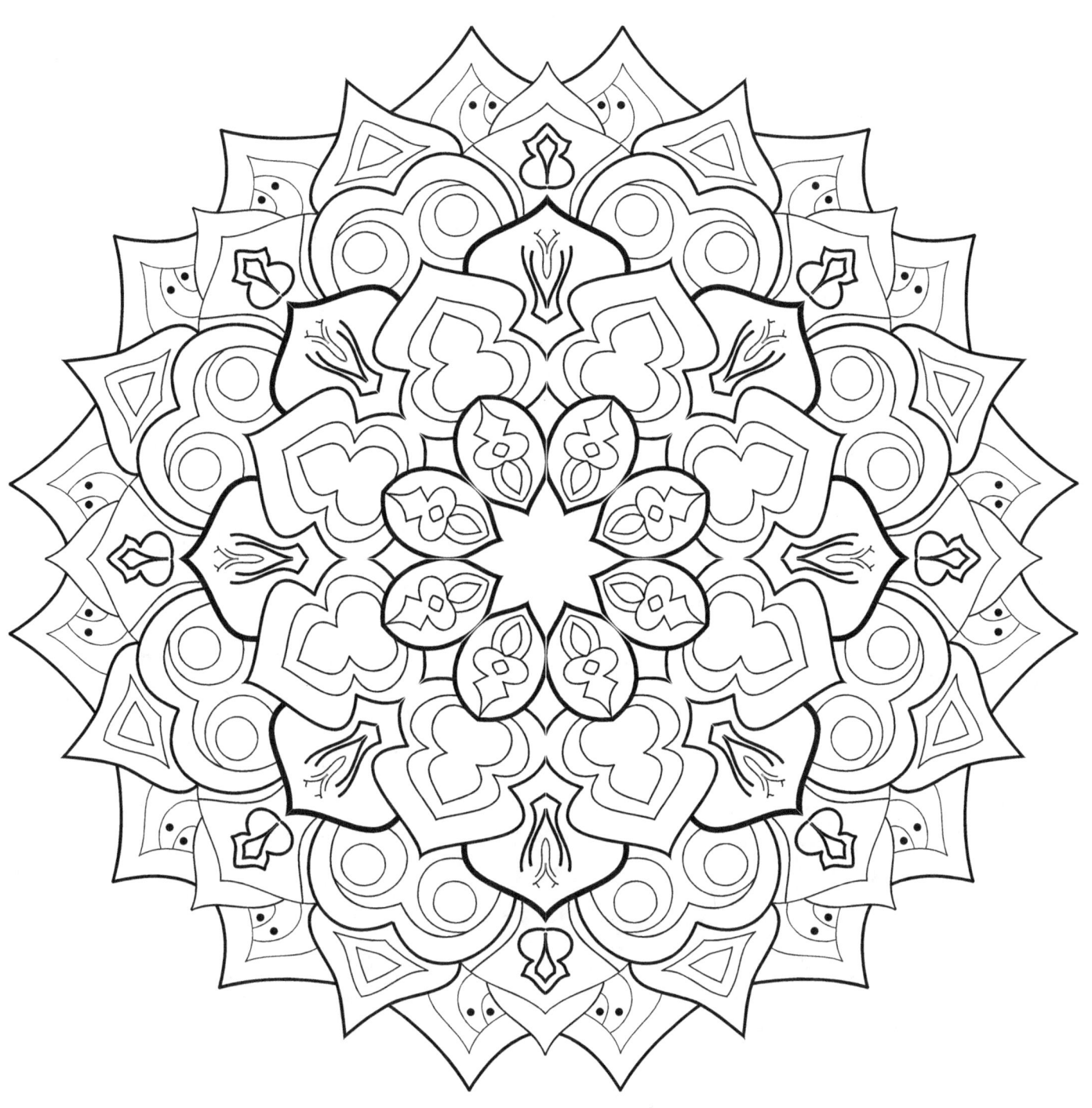

I WILL RUN & NOT GET TIRED

THE PEACE OF GOD, WHICH TRANSCENDS ALL UNDERSTANDING, WILL GUARD YOUR HEARTS AND YOUR MINDS IN CHRIST JESUS.

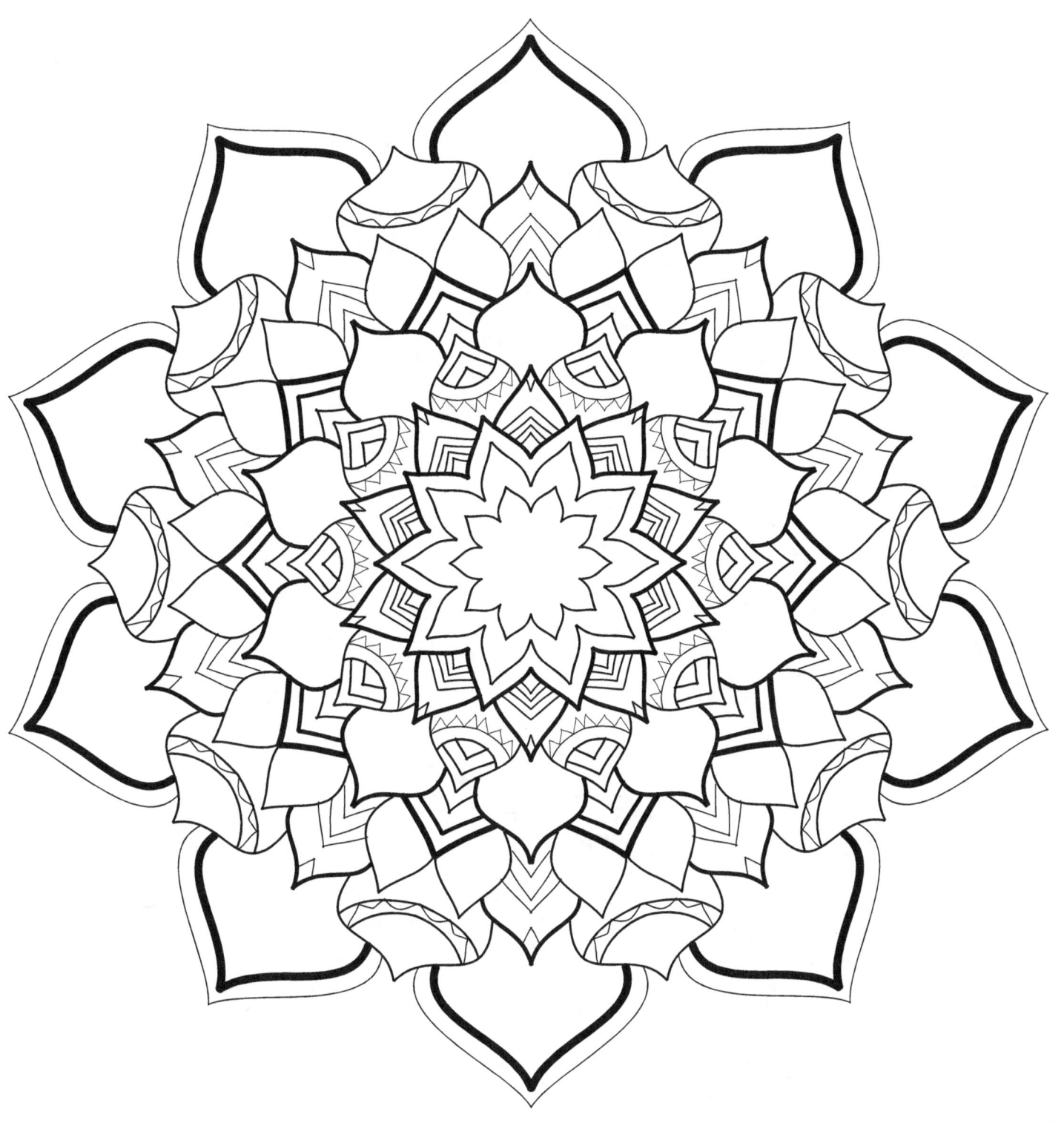

I WILL FEAR NO EVIL
FOR YOU ARE WITH ME

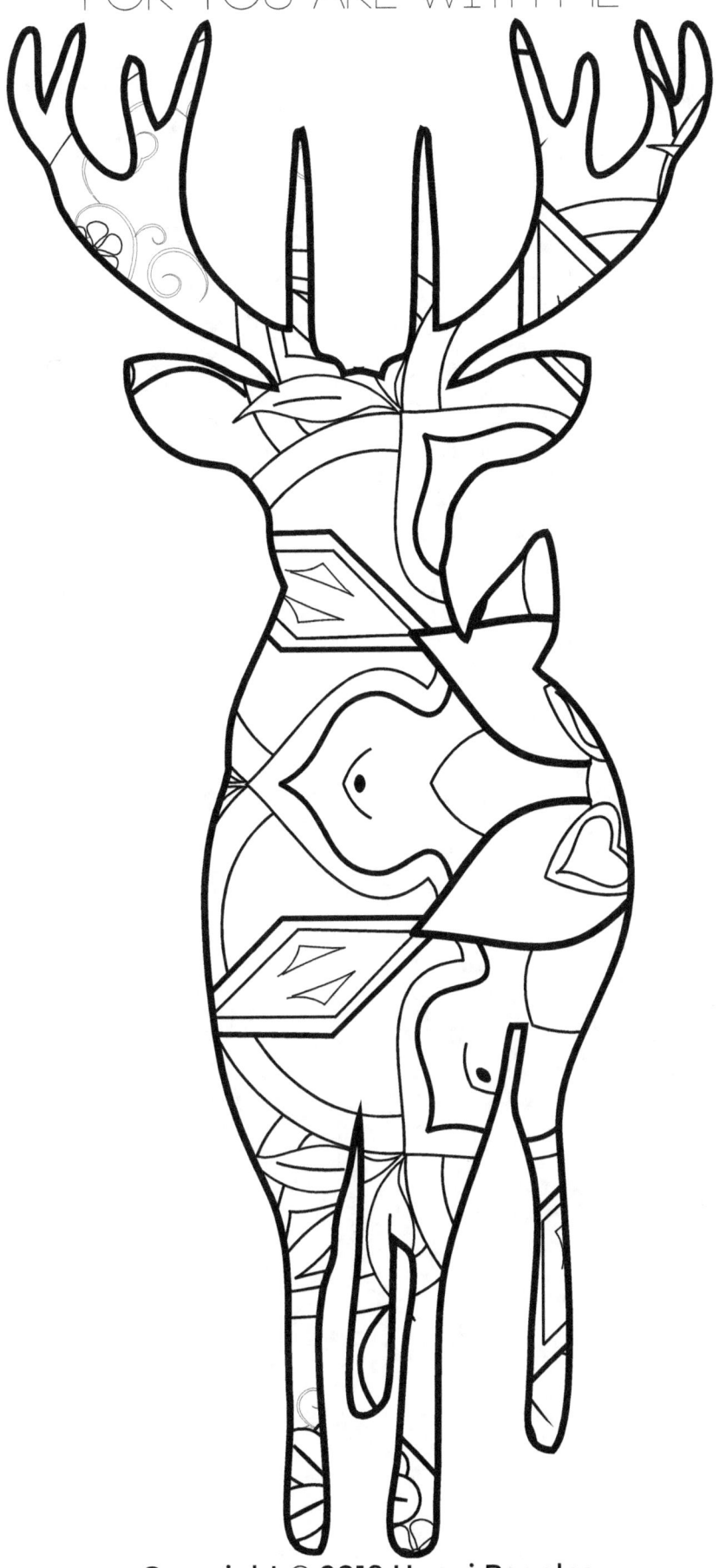

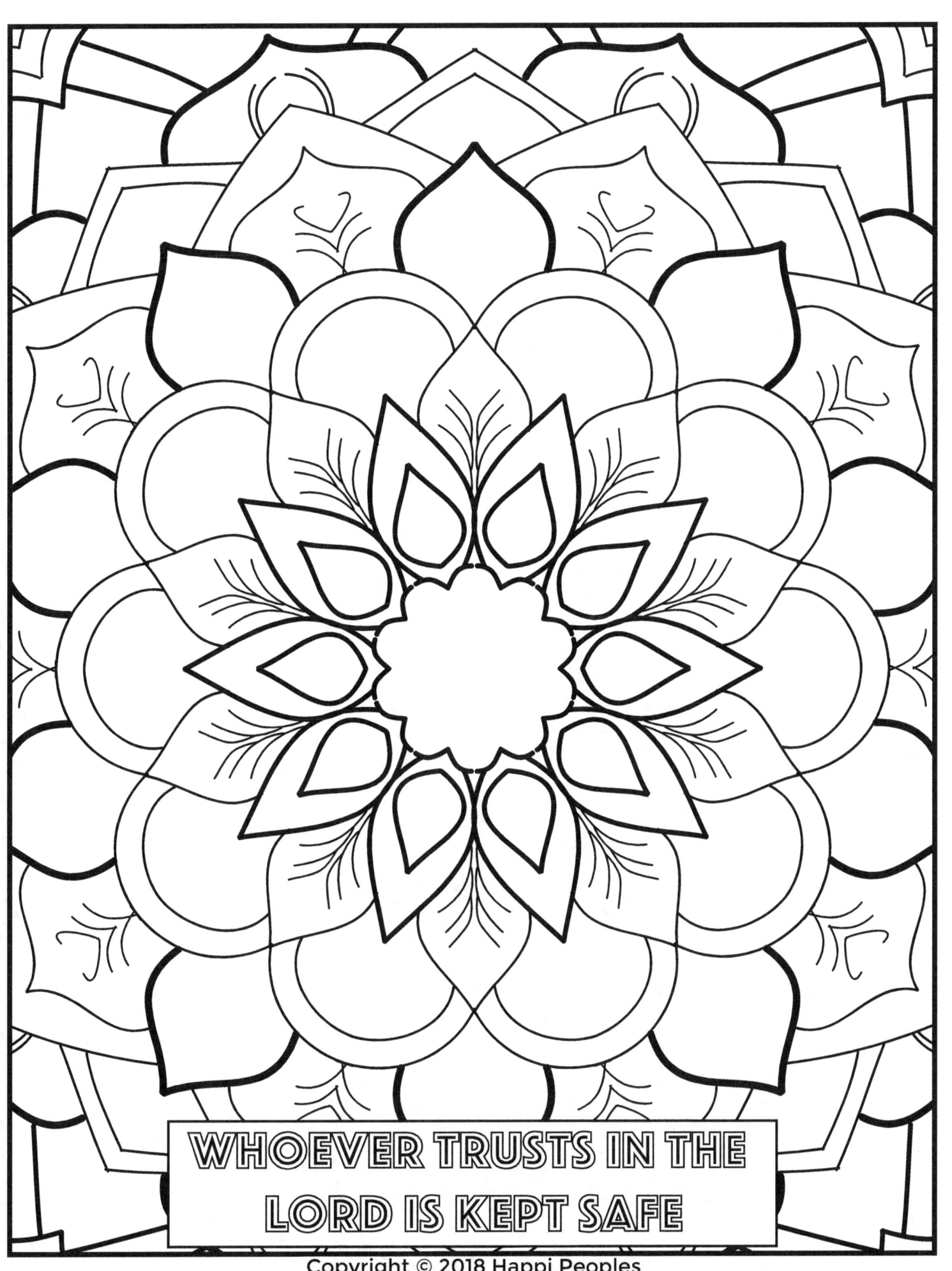

WHOEVER TRUSTS IN THE
LORD IS KEPT SAFE

Praise be to the God
who comforts us in all our troubles

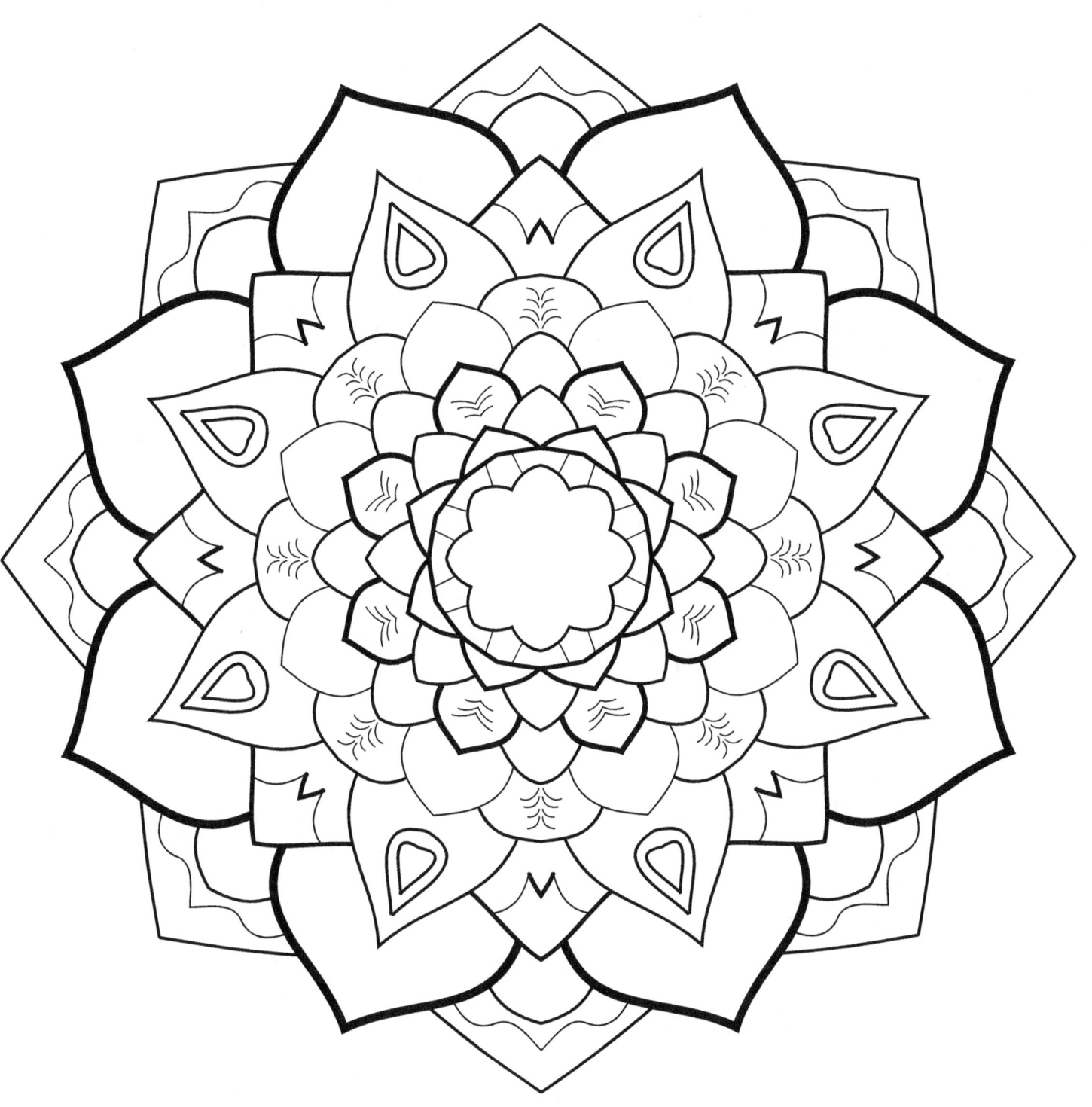

Do not let your hearts be troubled and do not be afraid.

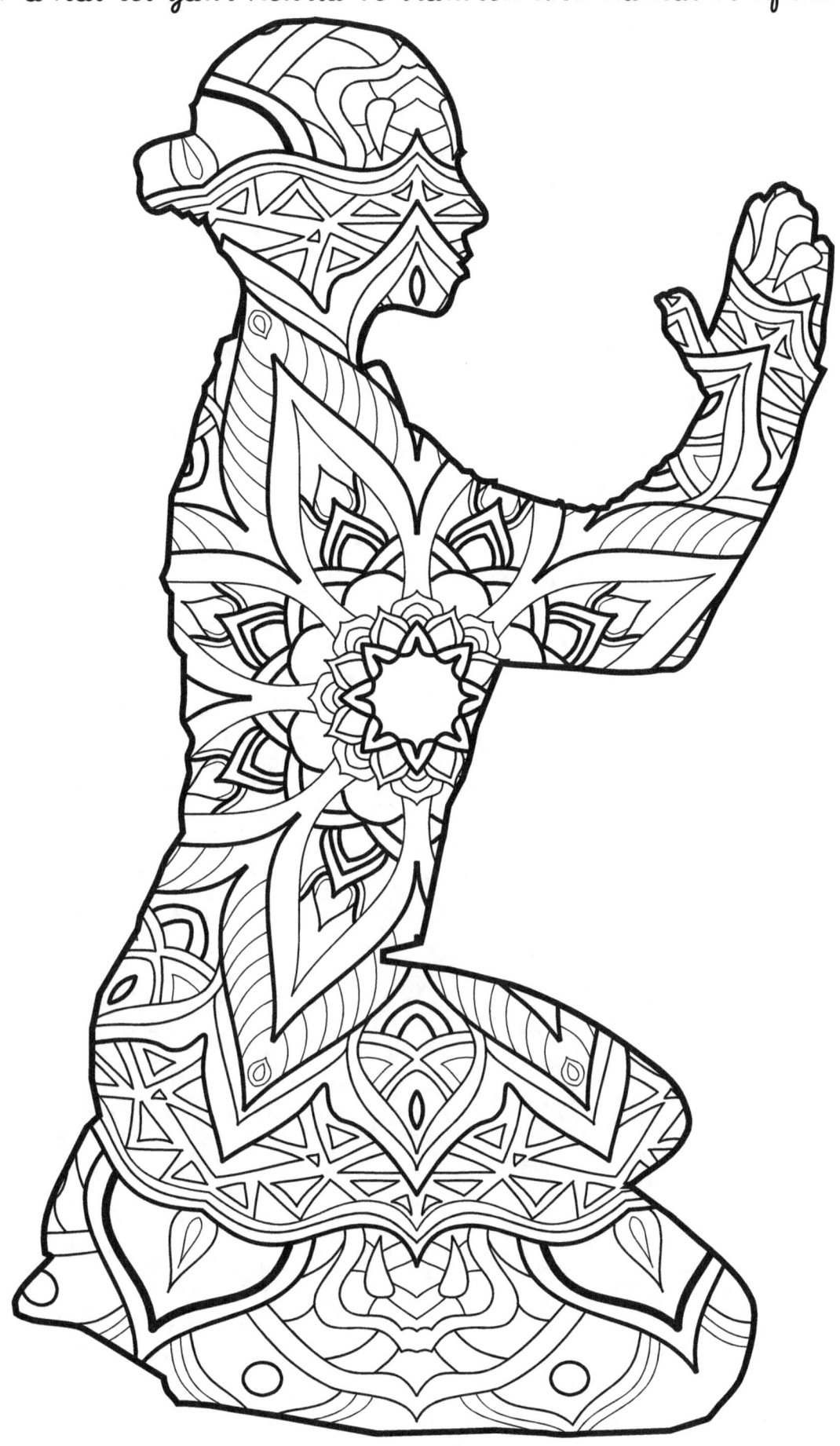

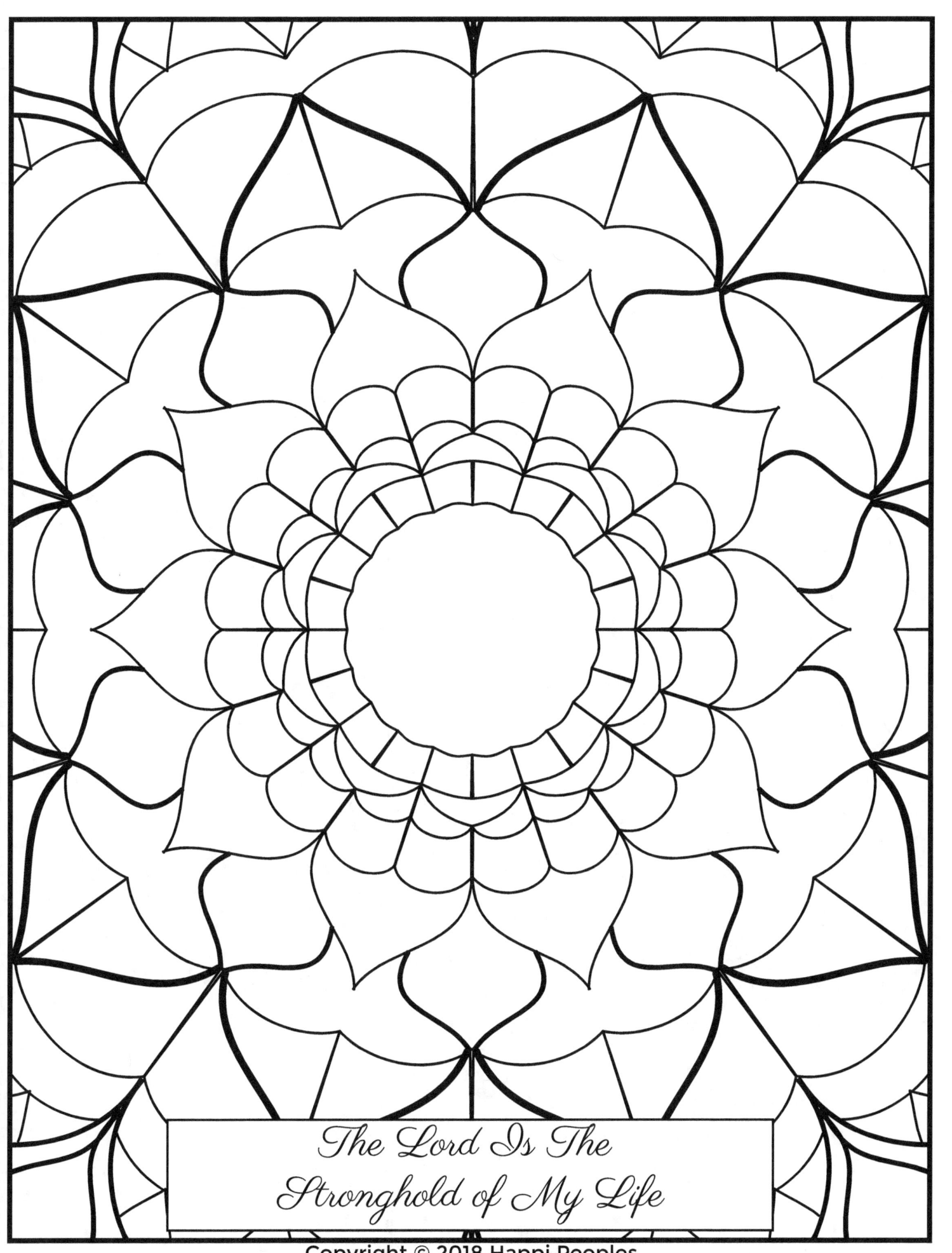

The Lord Is The
Stronghold of My Life

In every situation, by prayer, with thanksgiving, present your requests to God

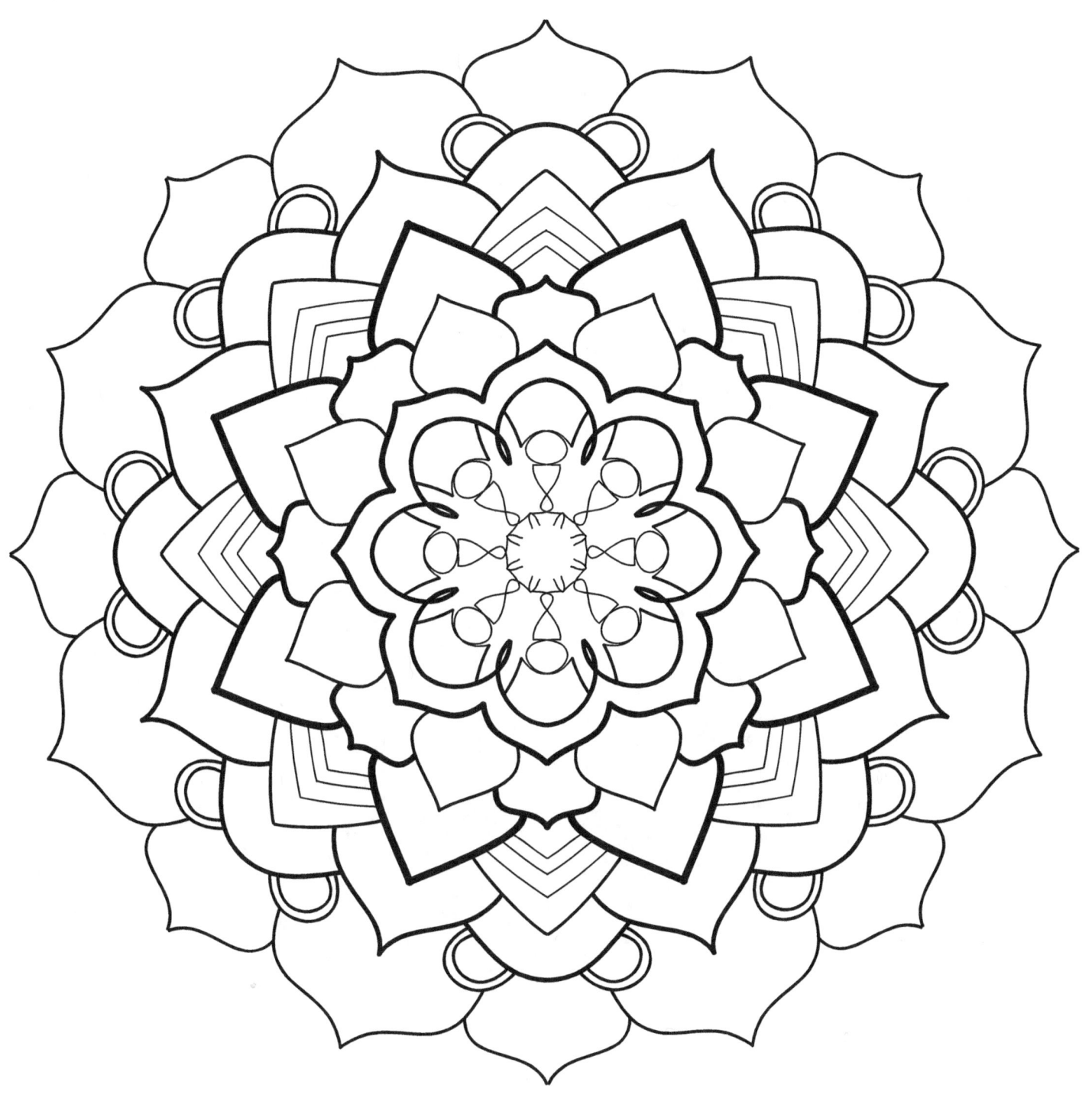

Renew My Strength Lord

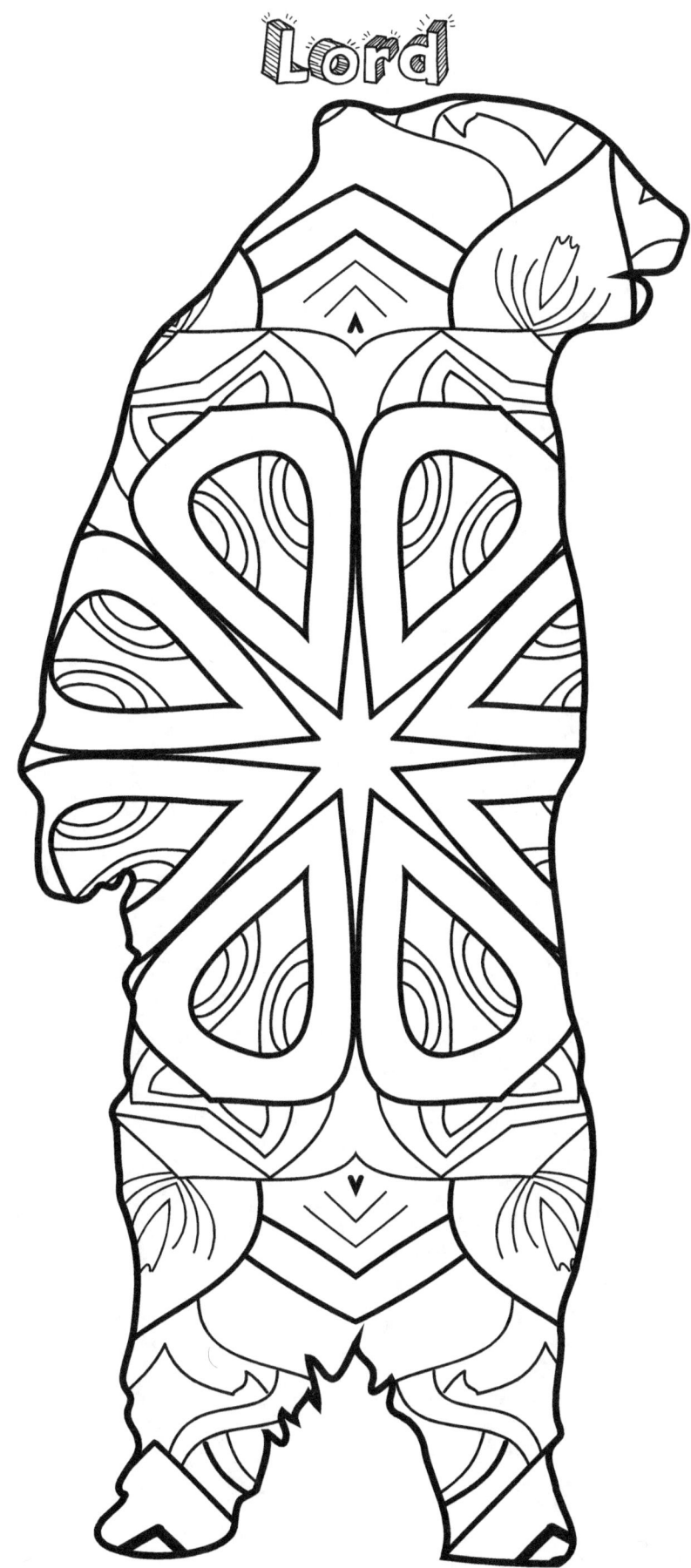

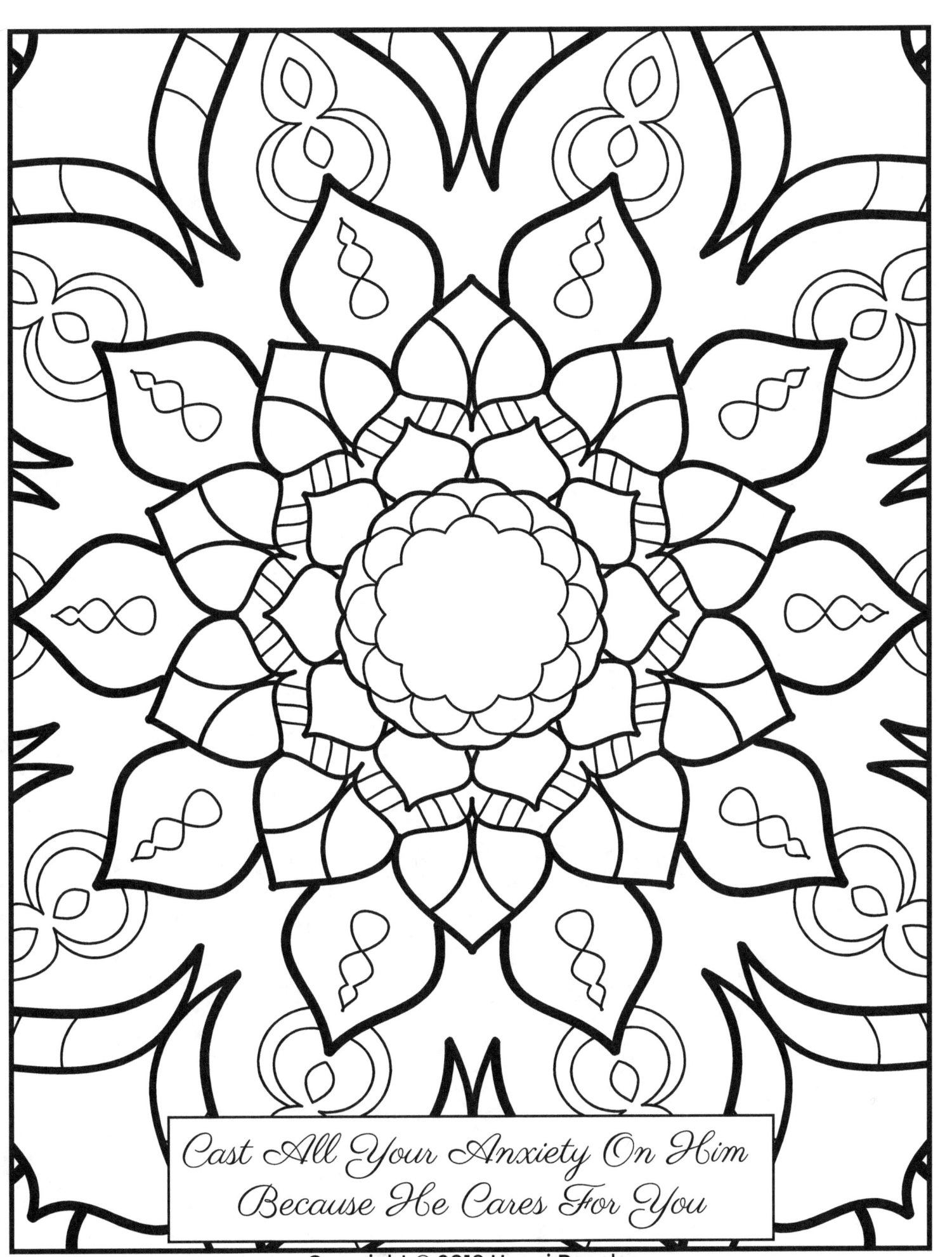

Cast All Your Anxiety On Him
Because He Cares For You

YOUR ROD & YOUR STAFF, THEY COMFORT ME.

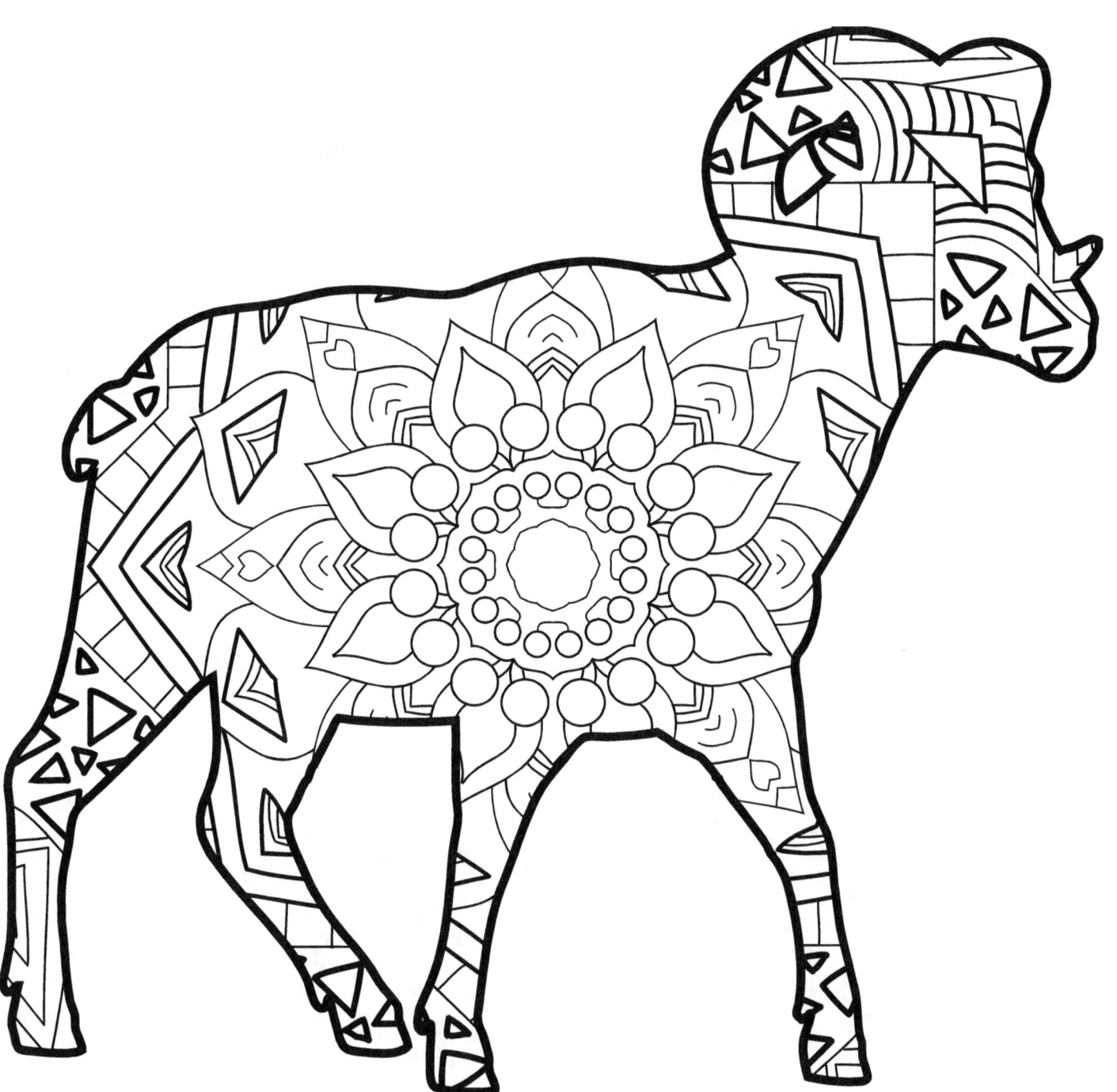

When you walk through the fire,
you will not be burned;
the flames will not set you ablaze.

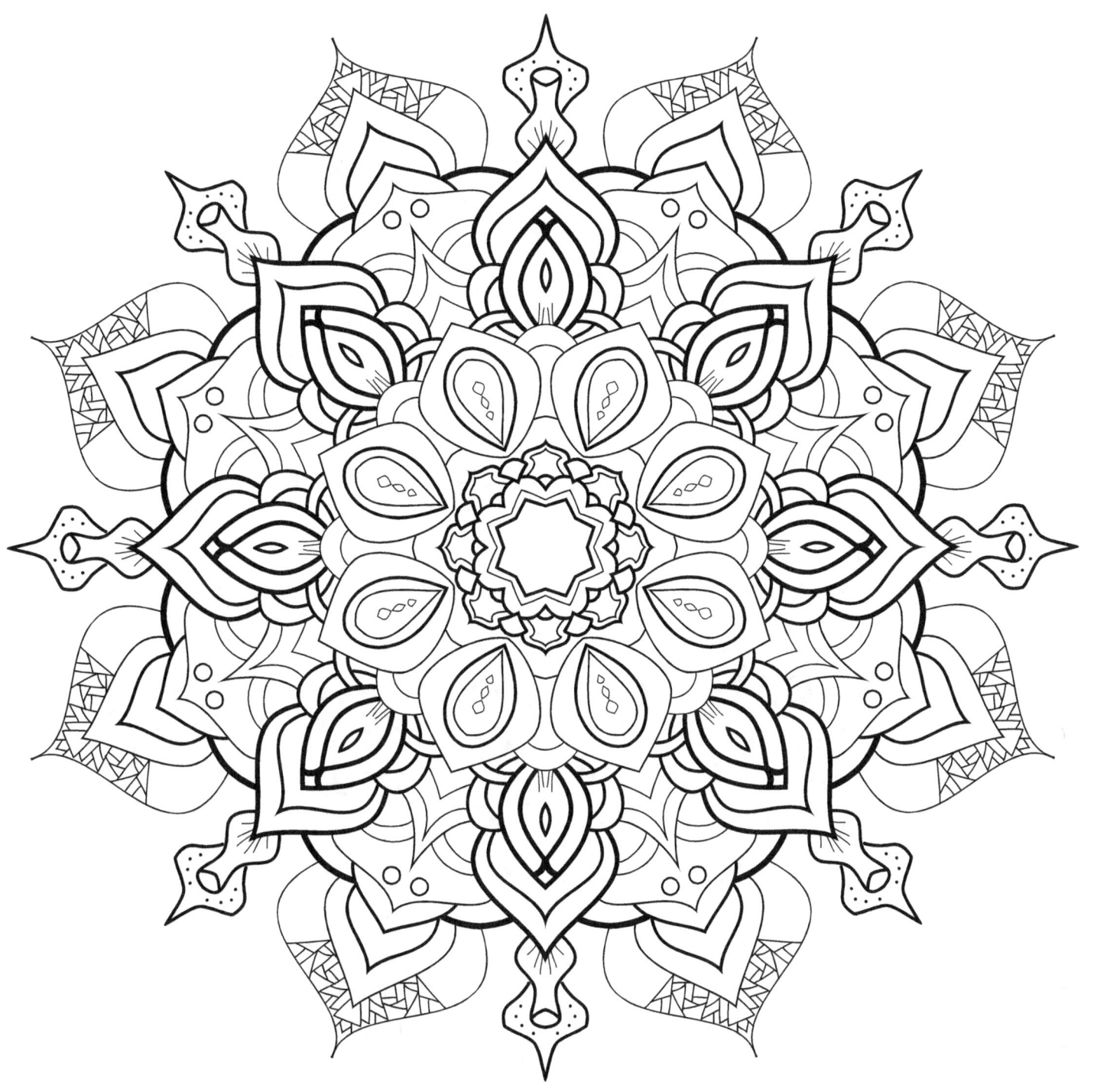

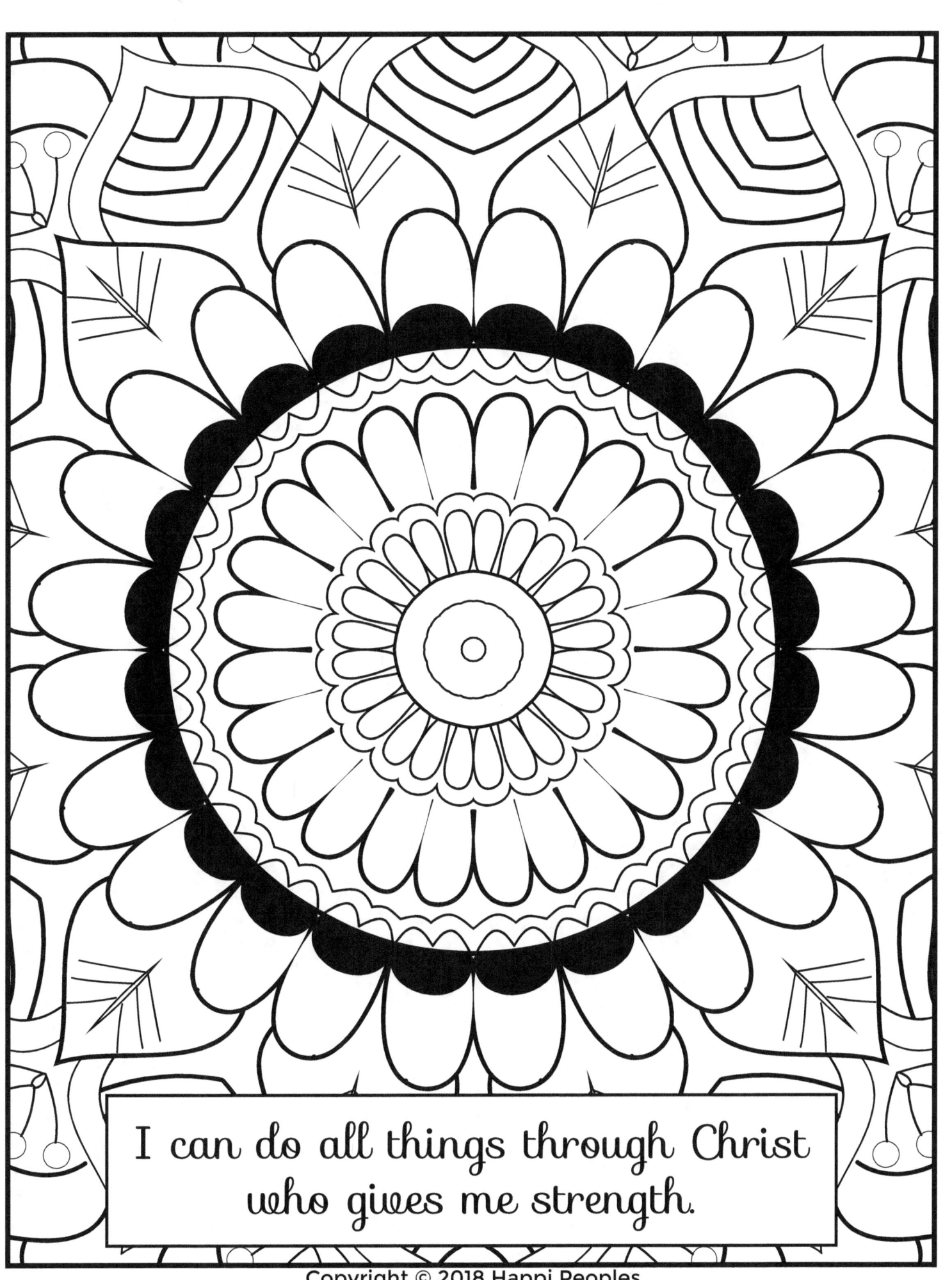

I can do all things through Christ
who gives me strength.

when you pass through the rivers,they will not sweep over you.

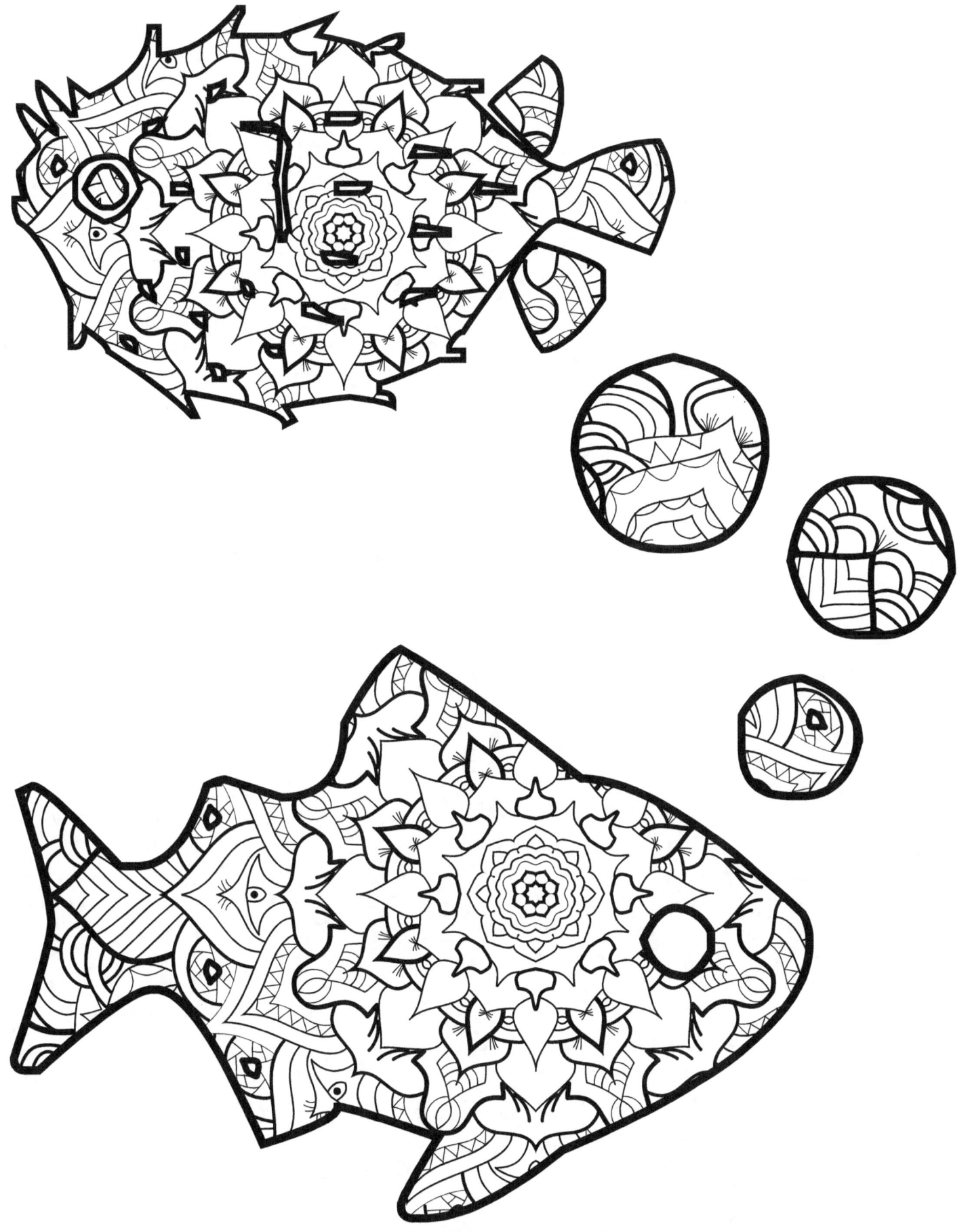

I will counsel you with my loving eye on you

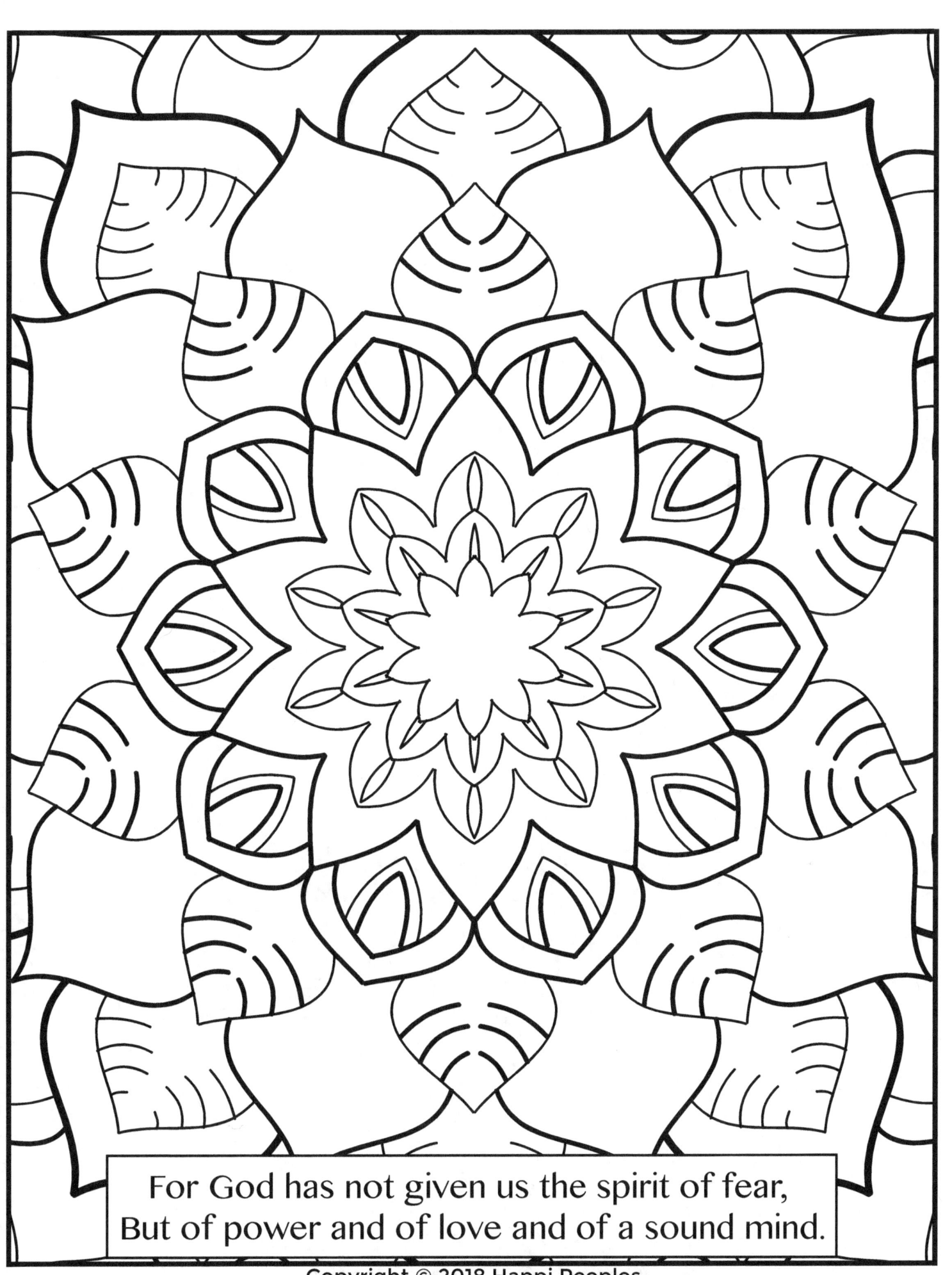

For God has not given us the spirit of fear,
But of power and of love and of a sound mind.

Come To Me, All You Who Are Weary & Burdened & I Will Give You Rest.

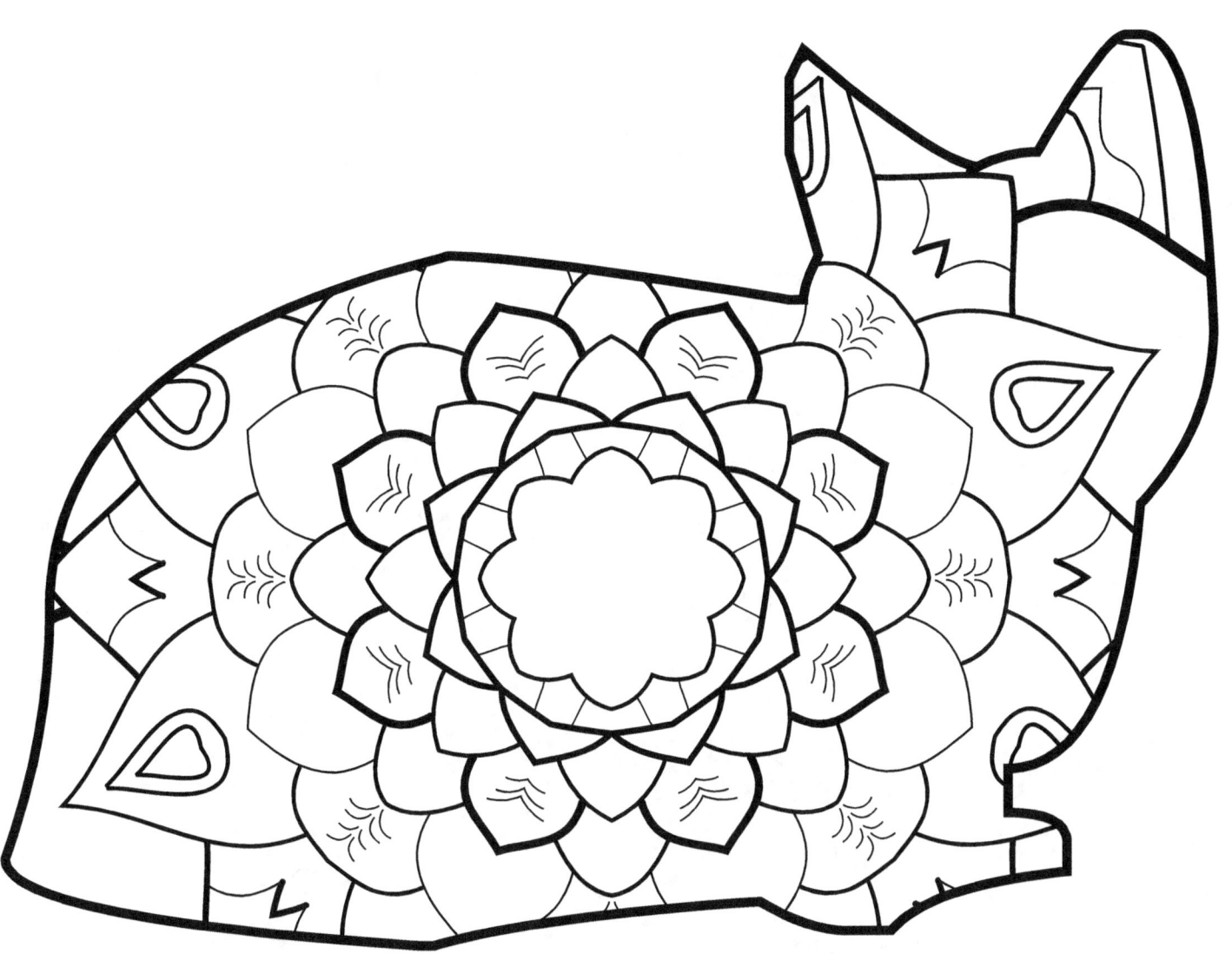

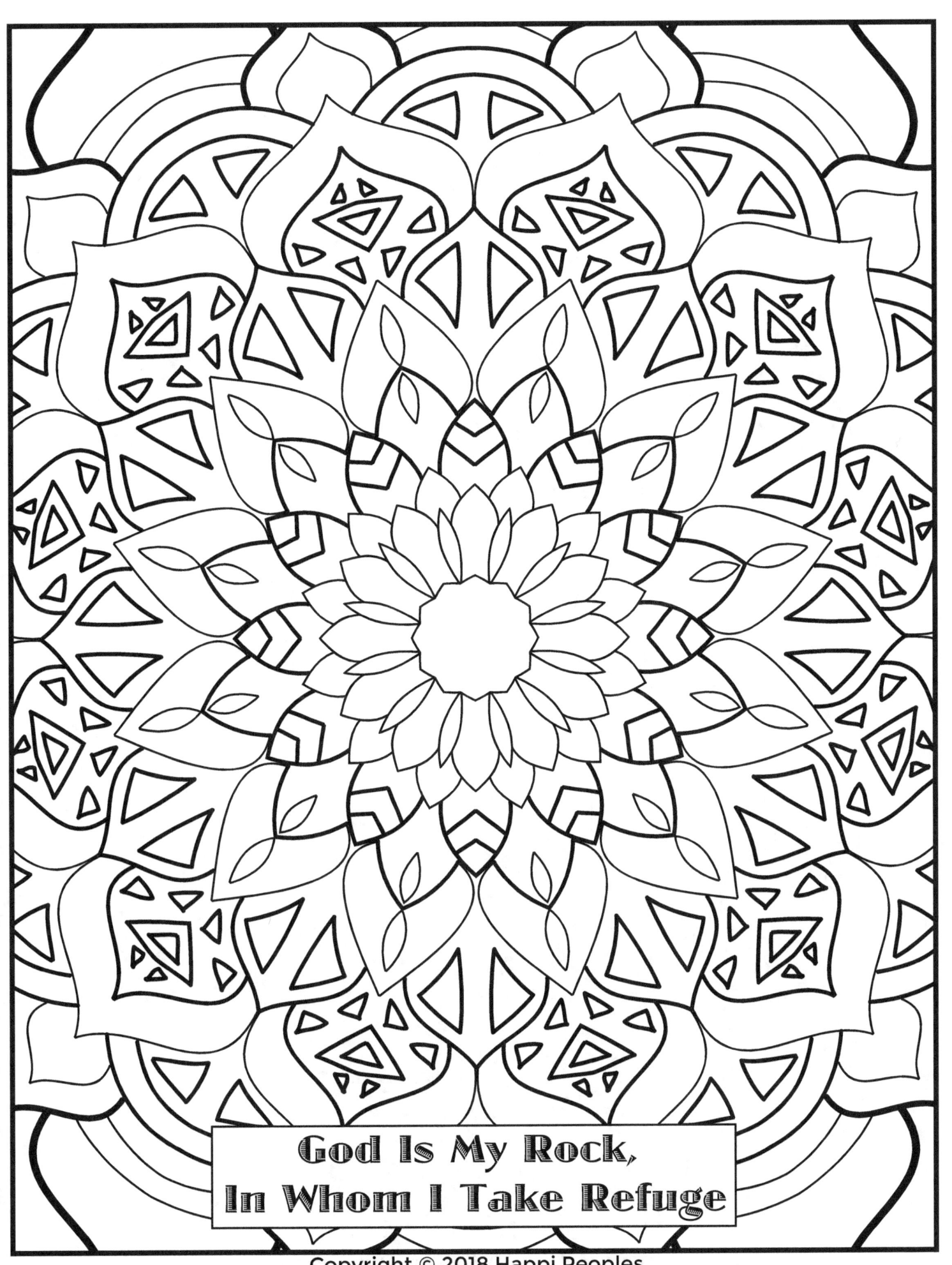

God Is My Rock,
In Whom I Take Refuge

Be Encouraged

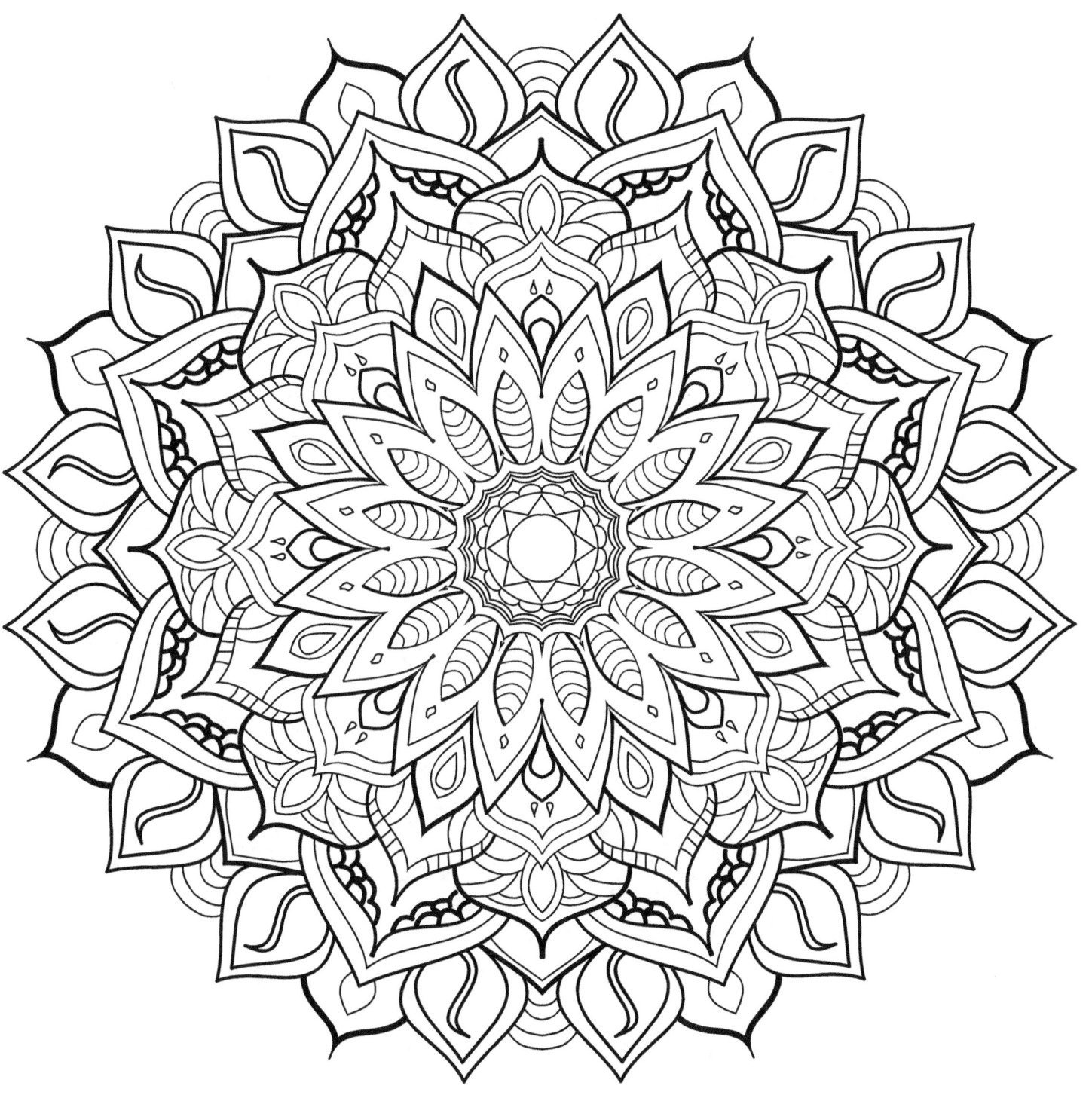

Peace I Leave With You;
My Peace I Give You

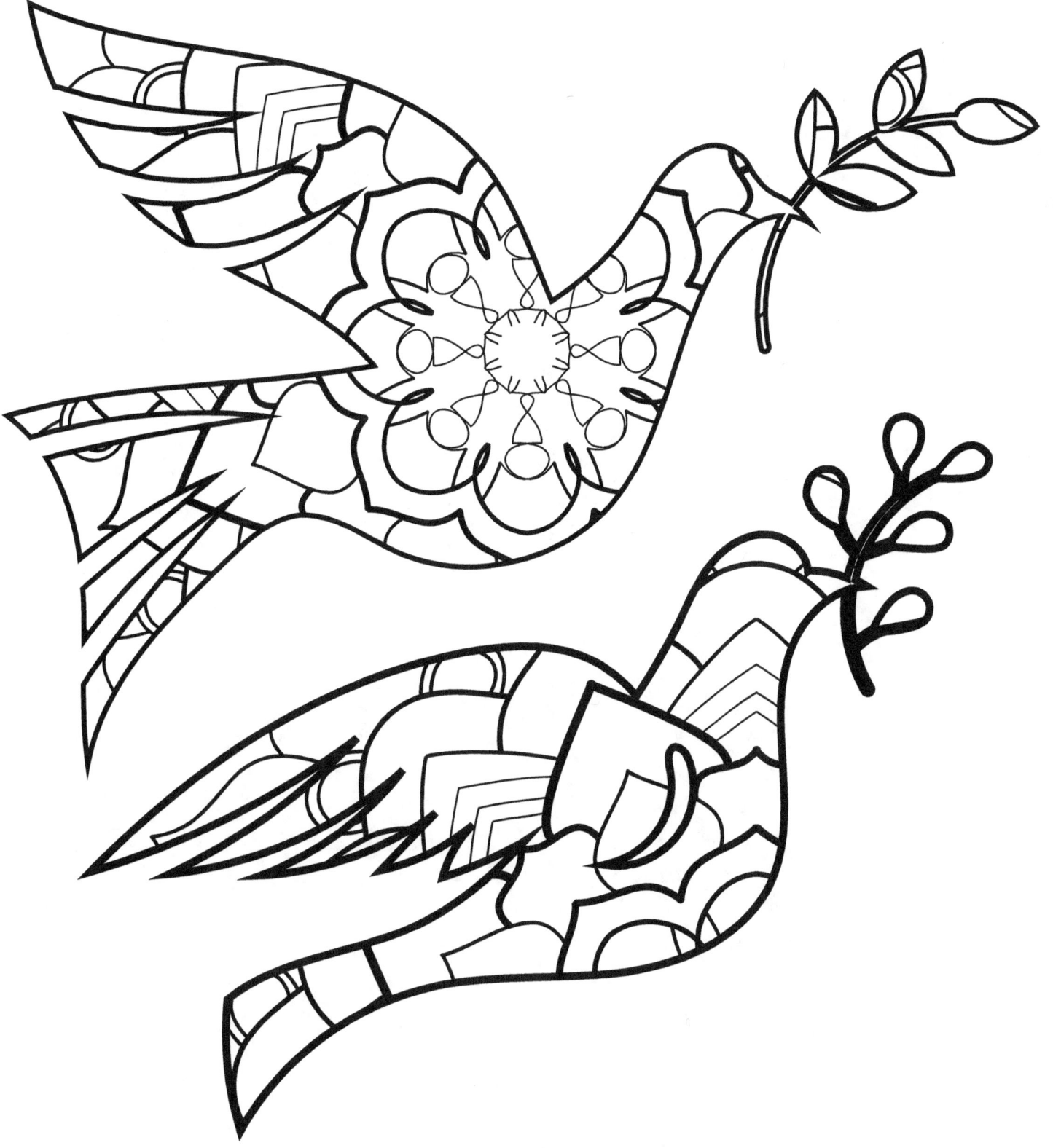

FOR I AM THE LORD YOUR GOD, WHO TAKES HOLD OF YOUR RIGHT HAND AND SAYS TO YOU, DO NOT FEAR; I WILL HELP YOU.

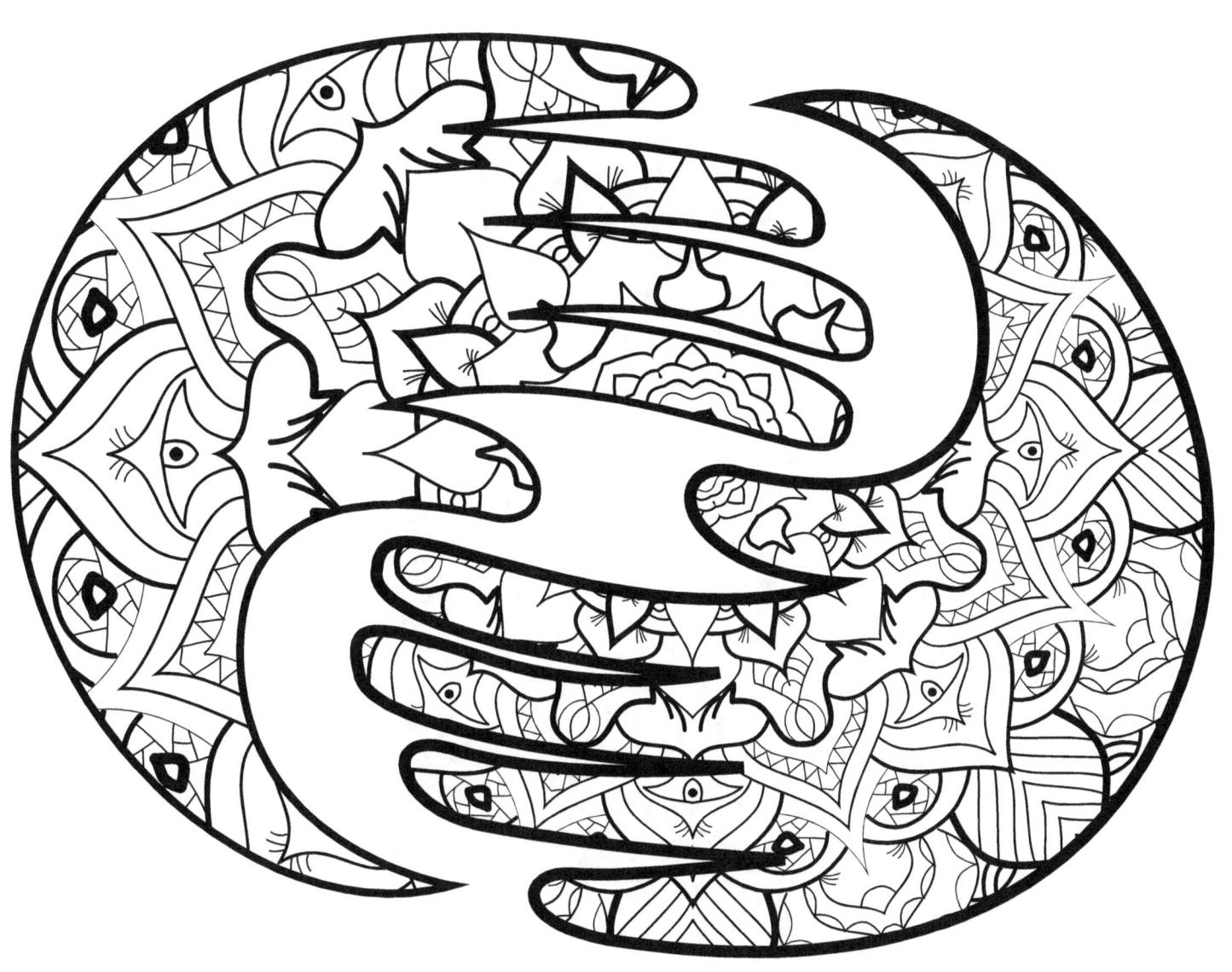

My Help Comes From The Lord

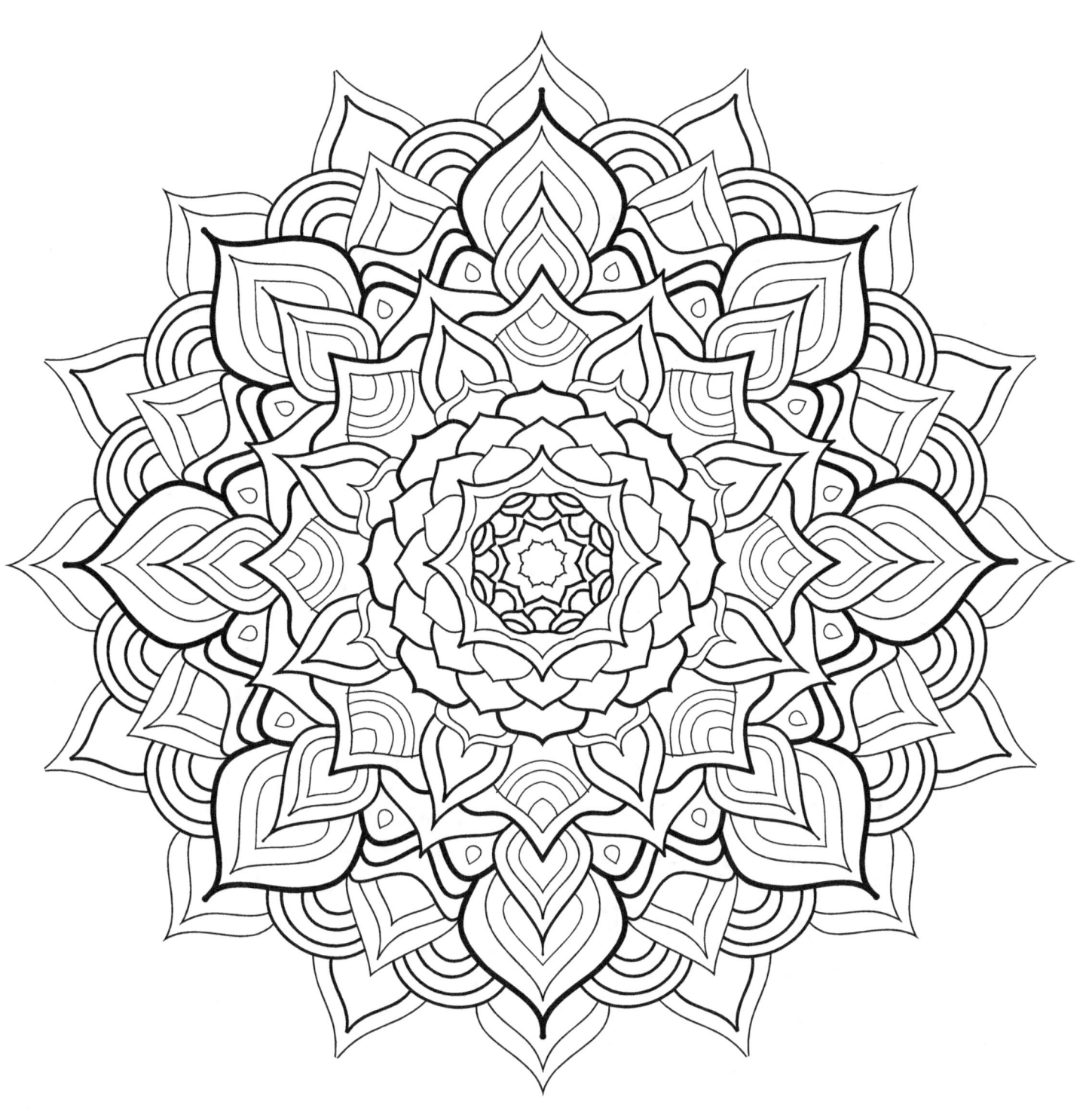

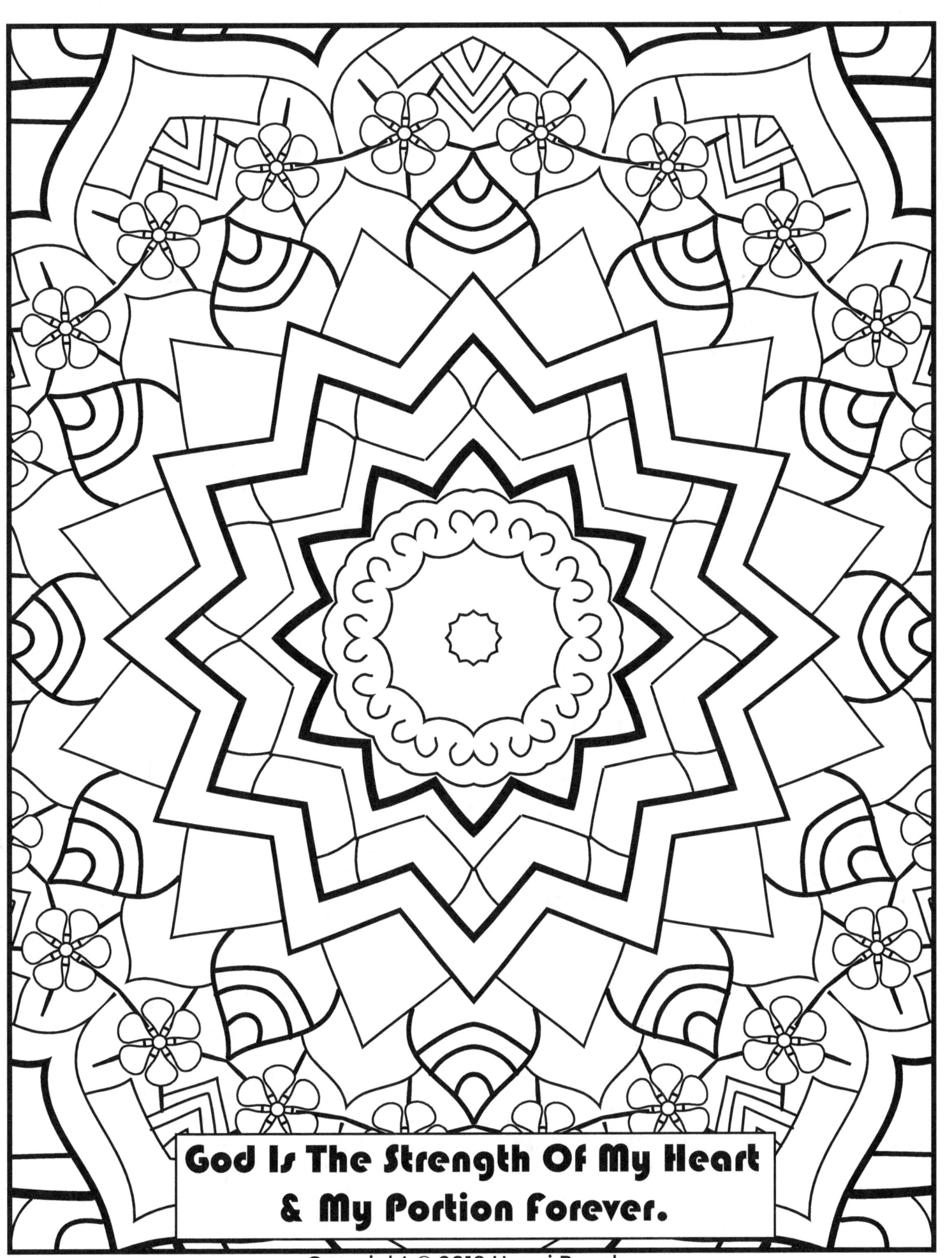

God Is The Strength Of My Heart
& My Portion Forever.

When I am afraid, I put my trust in you.

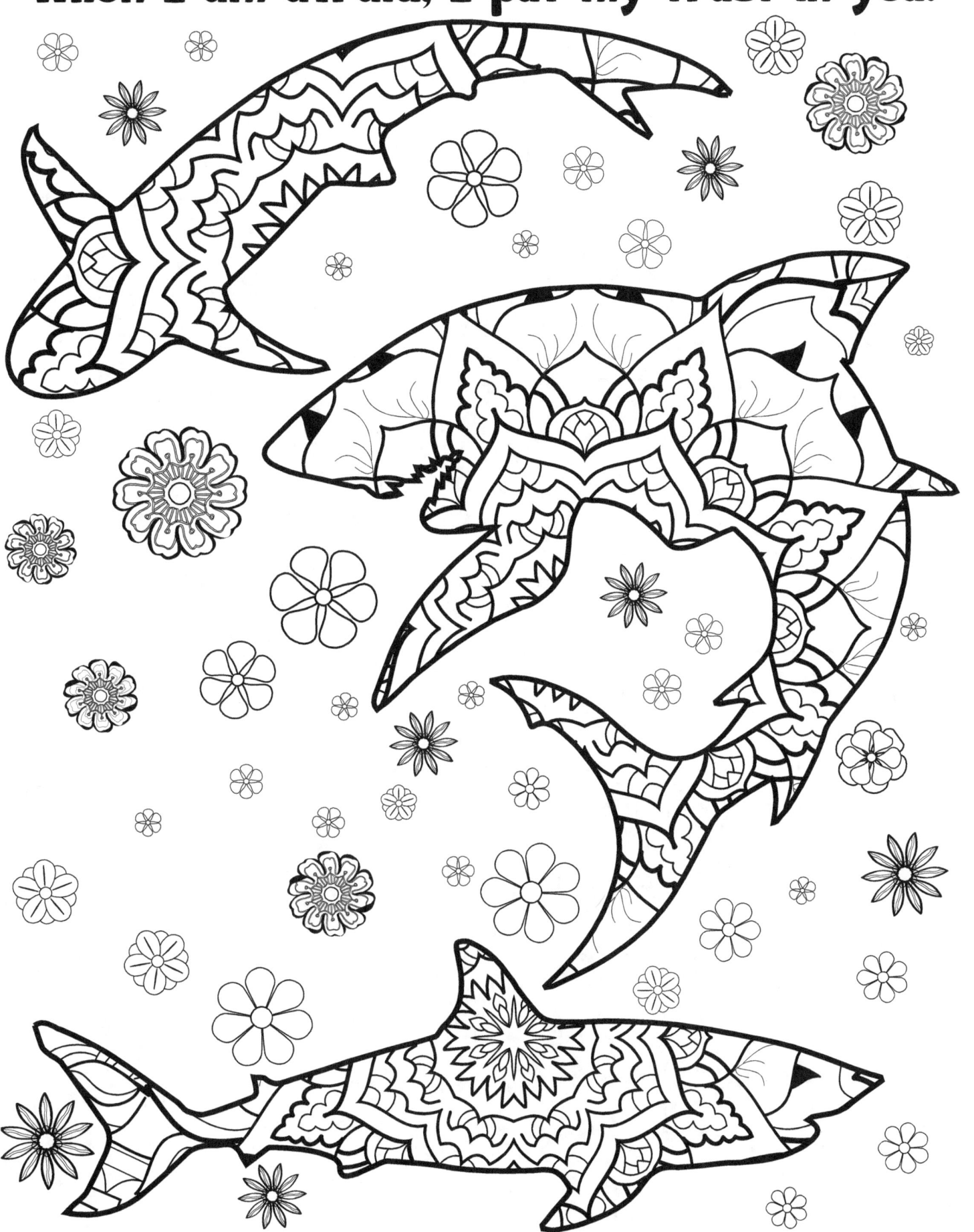

The Lord is my light & my salvation

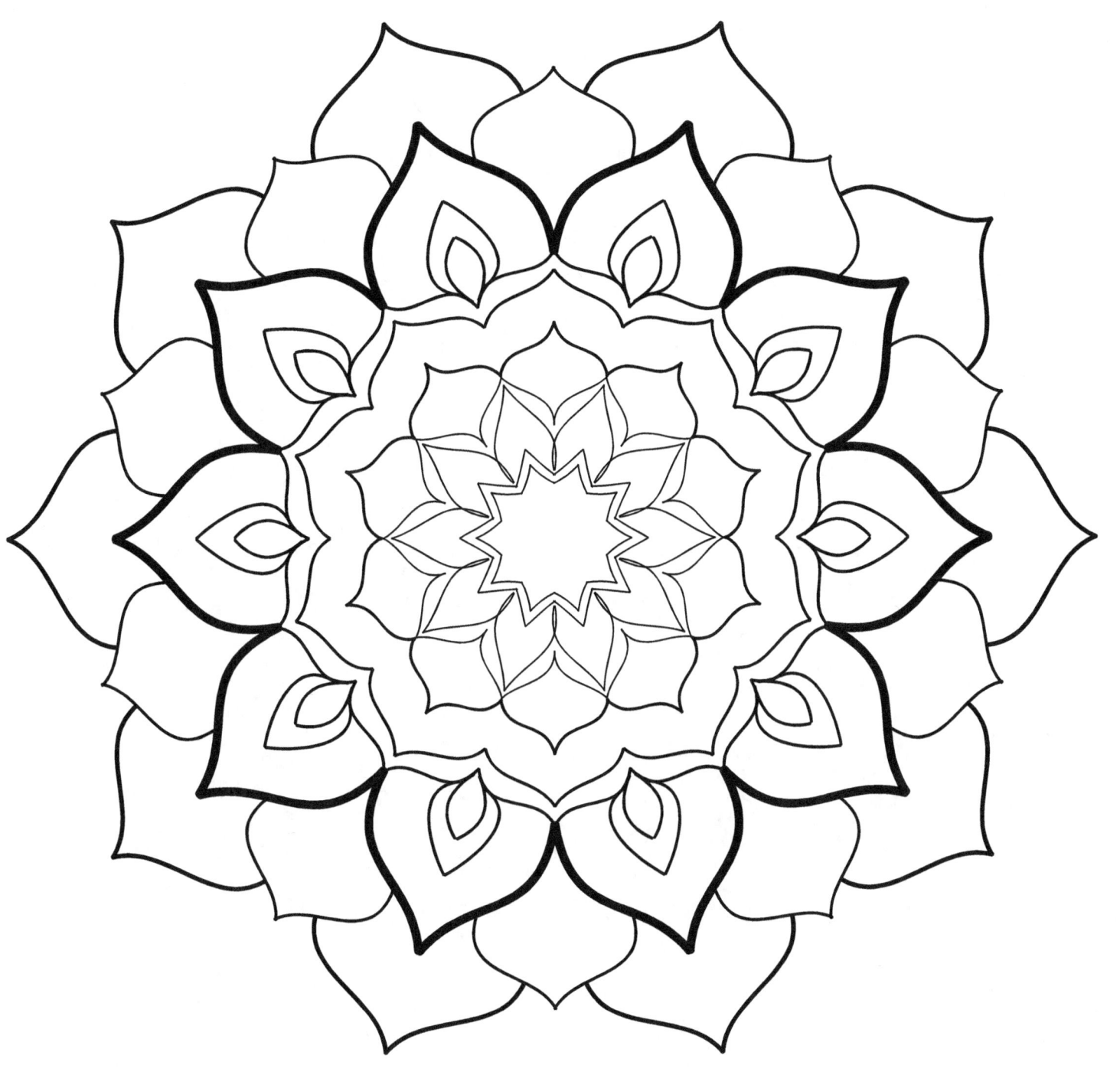

I will strengthen you & help you;
I will uphold you with my
righteous hand.

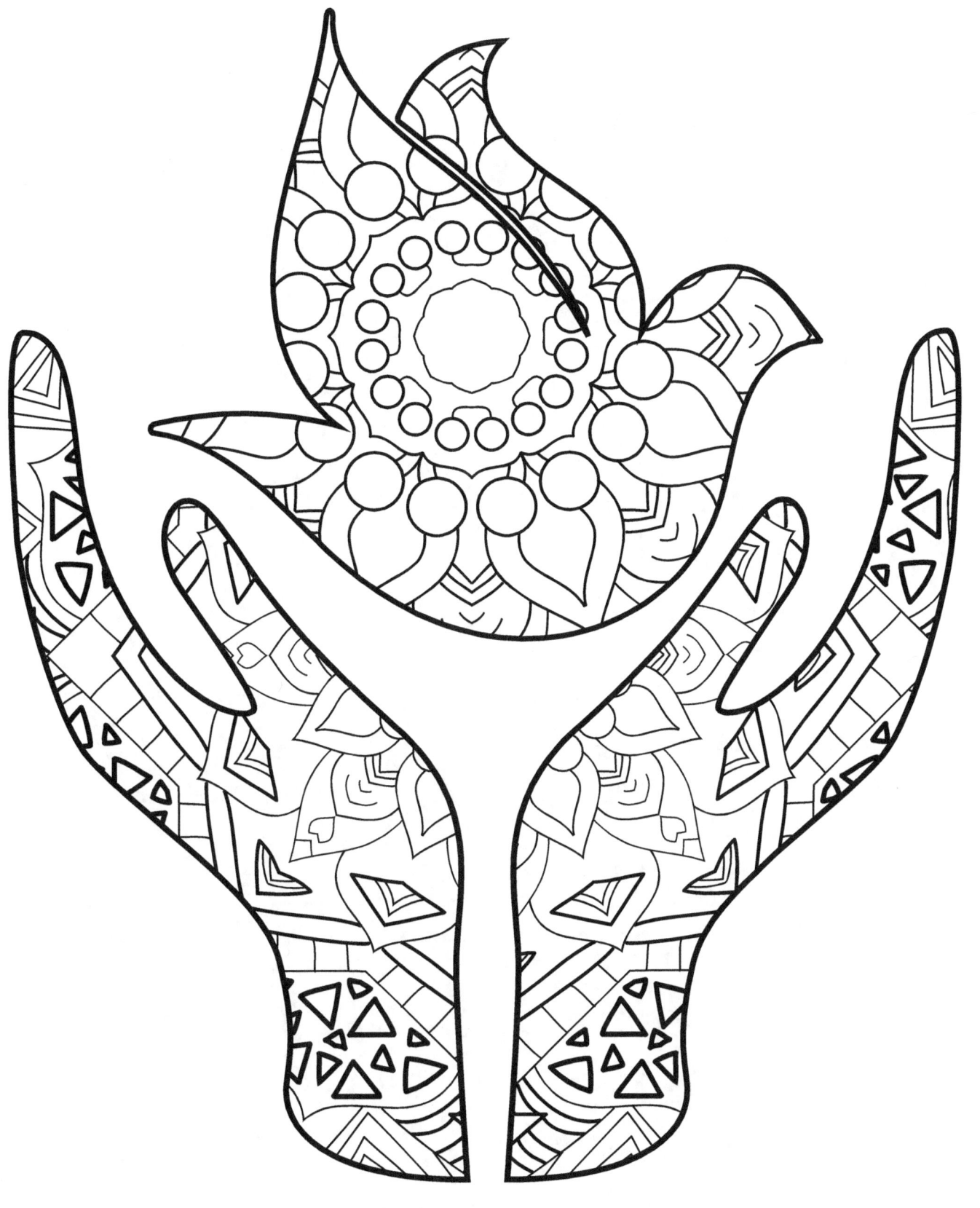

Do Not Be Anxious About Anything

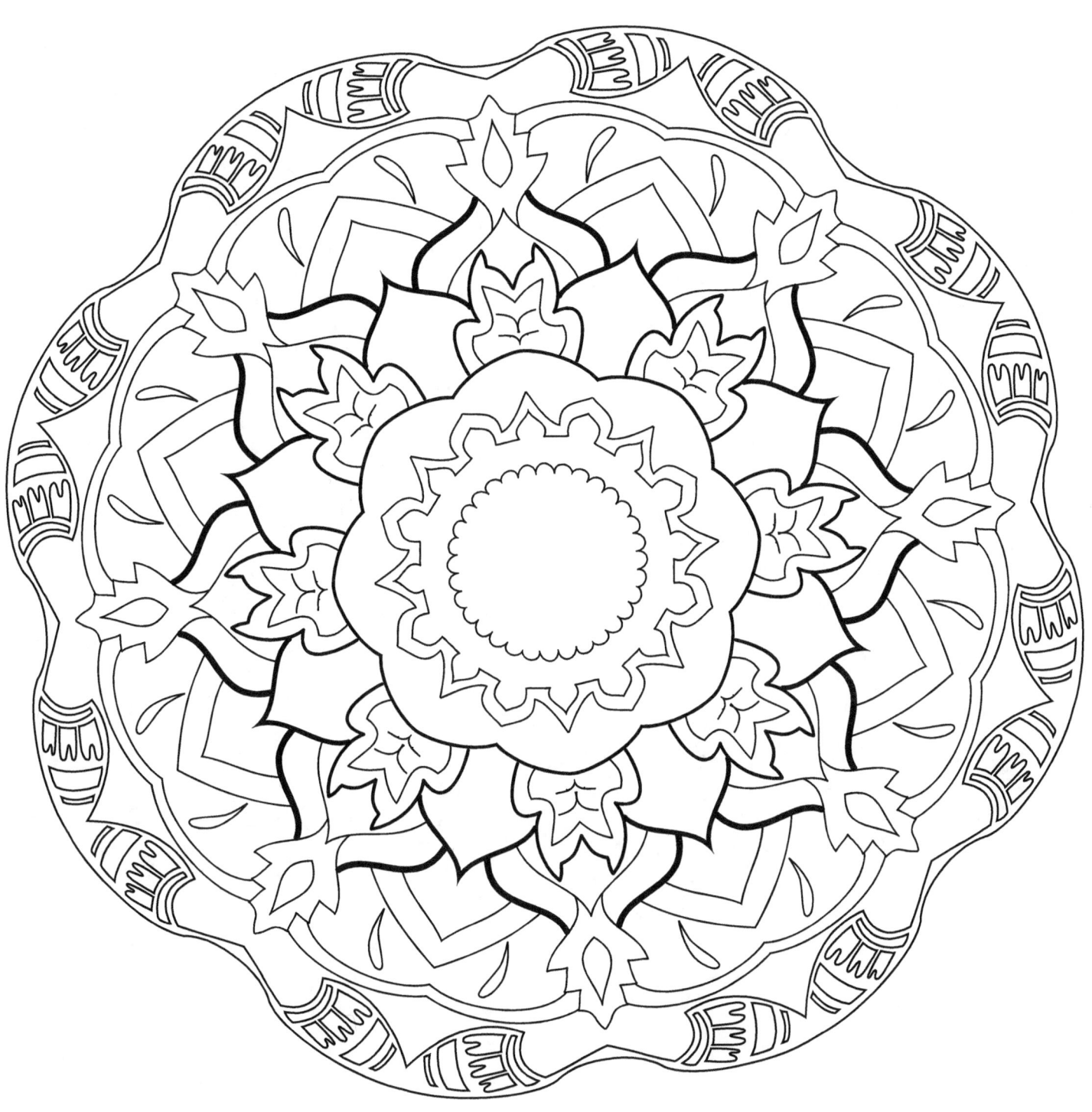

The Lord is with me; I will not be afraid.

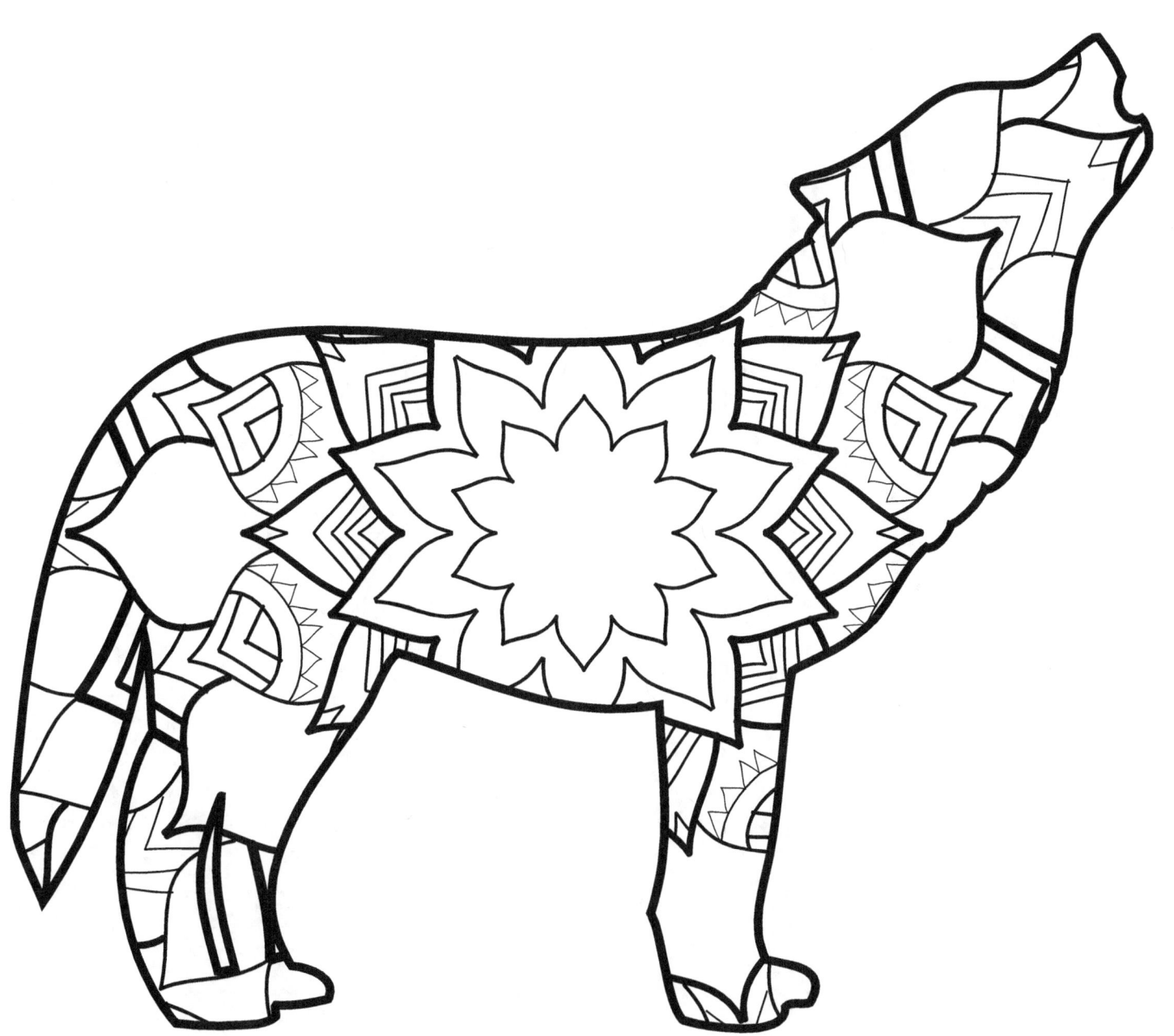

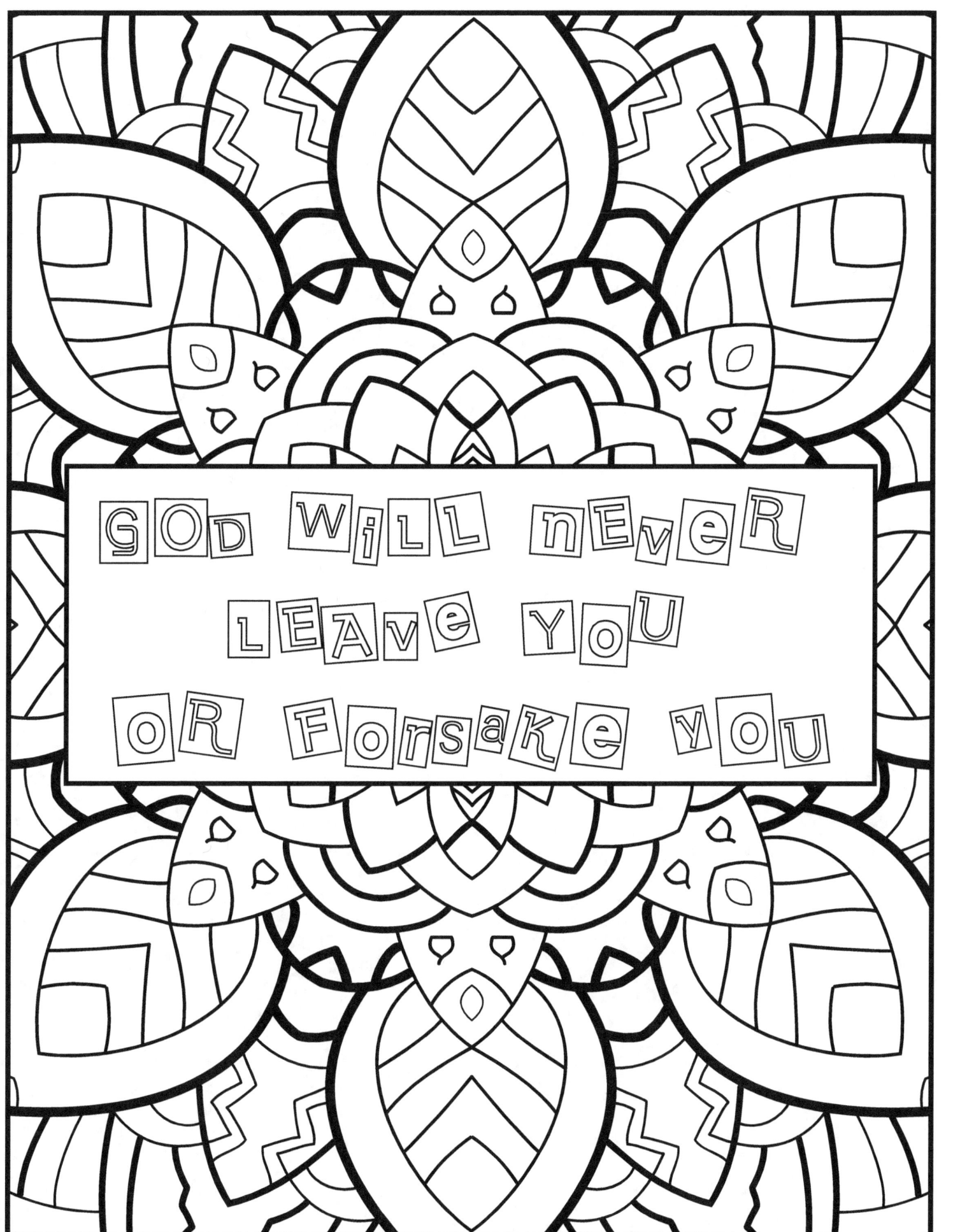

THERE IS NO FEAR IN LOVE.
BUT PERFECT LOVE DRIVES OUT FEAR

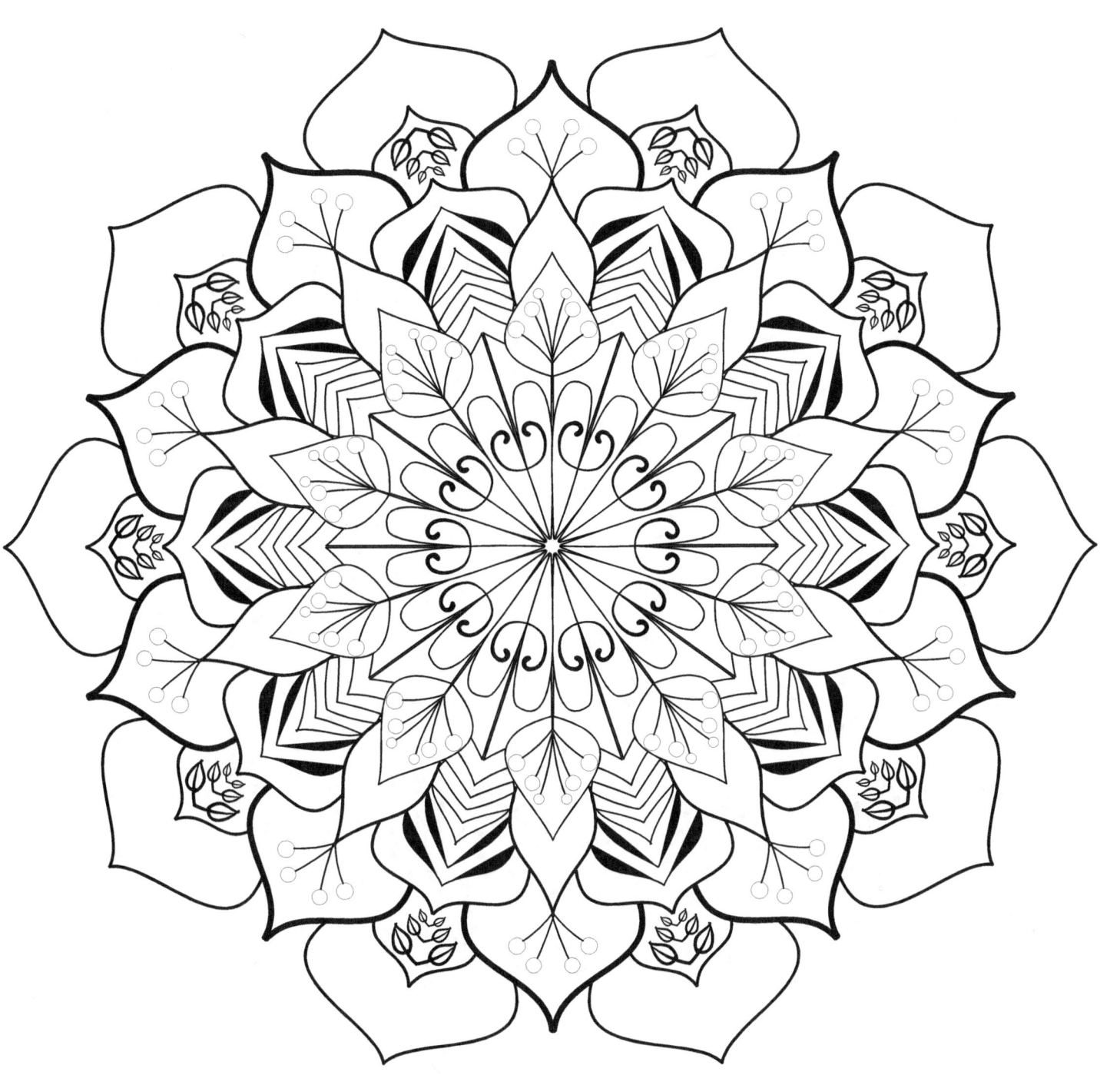

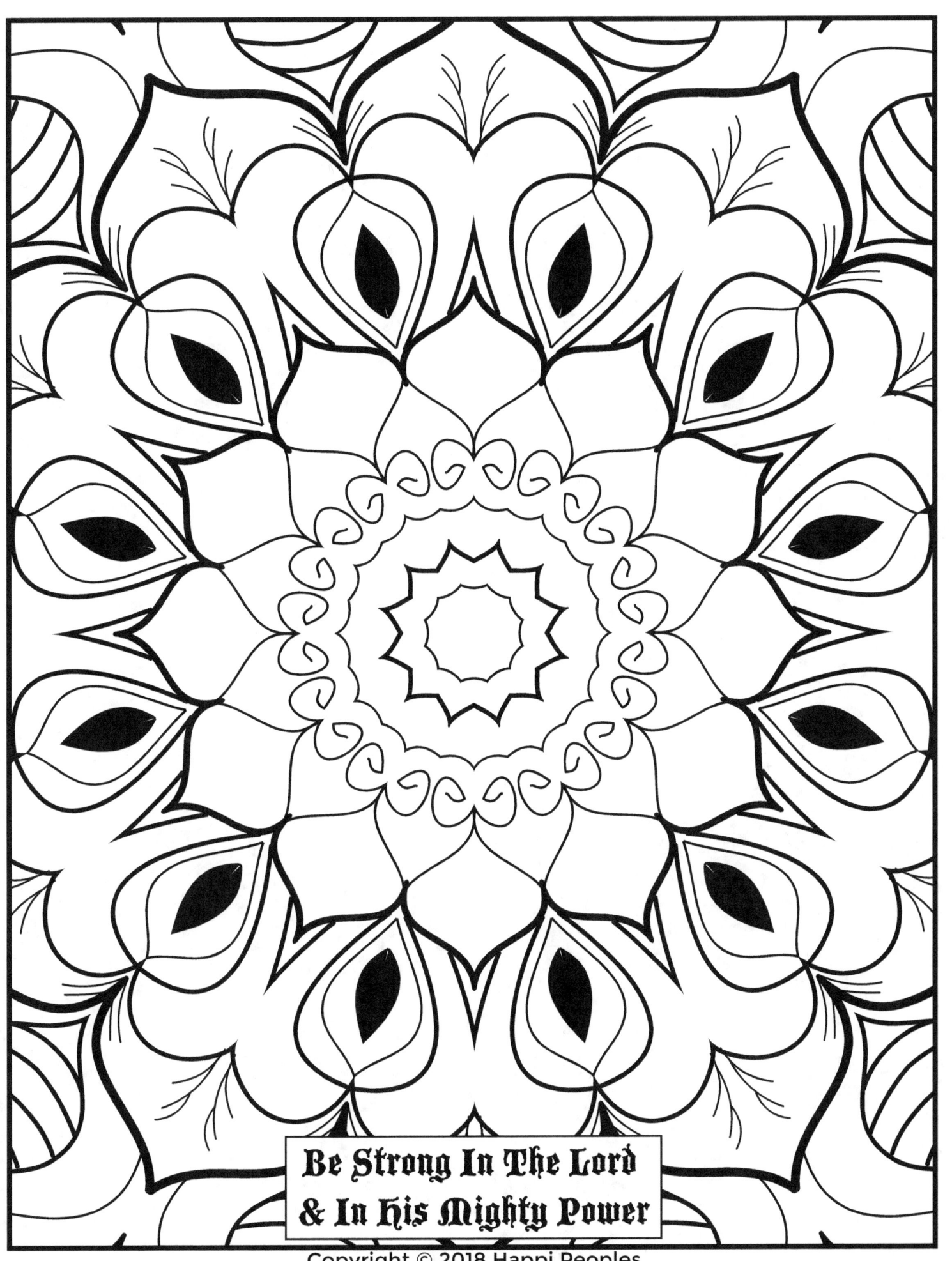

Be Strong In The Lord
& In His Mighty Power

BE STRONG AND TAKE HEART ALL YOU WHO HOPE IN THE LORD

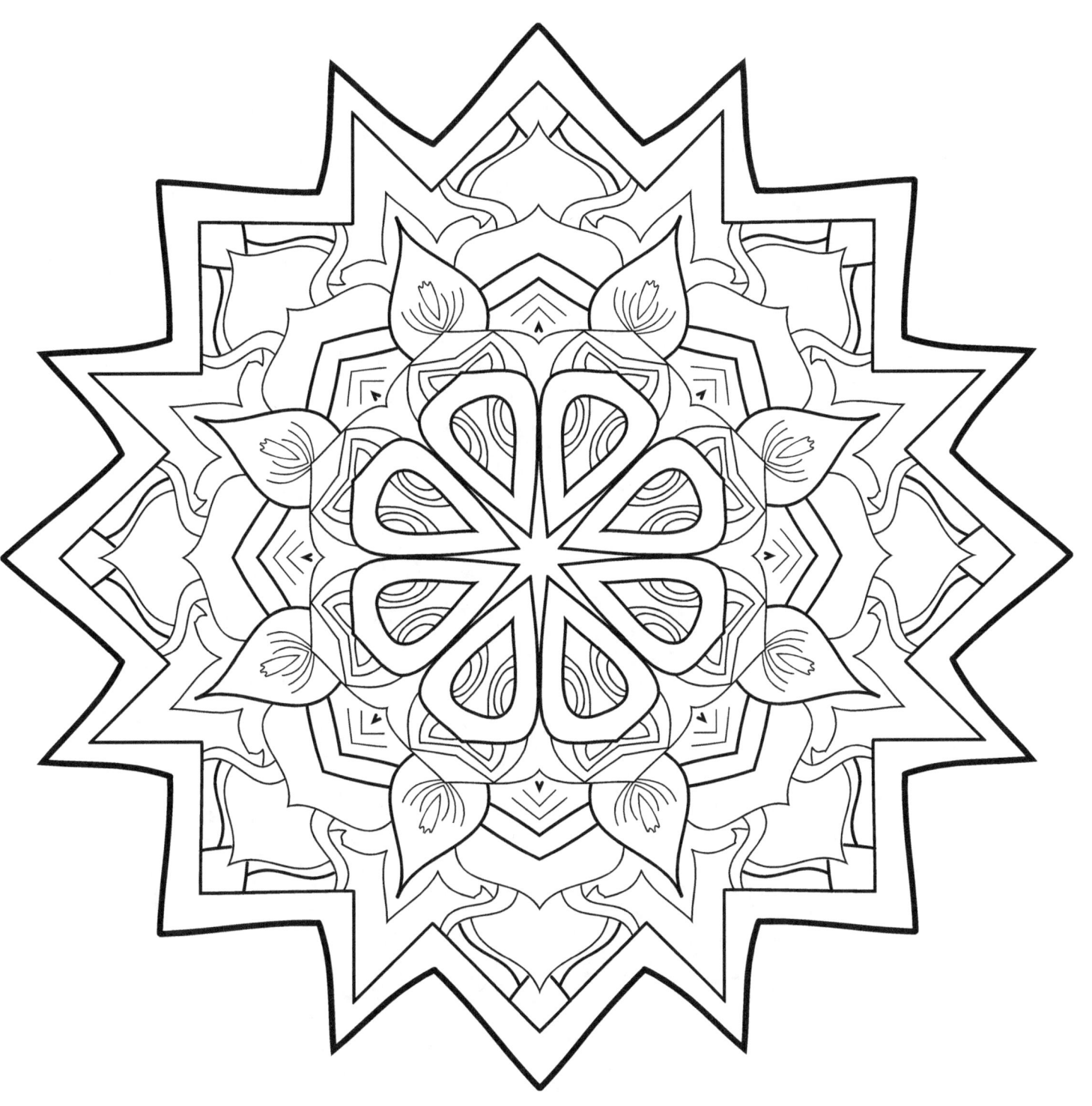

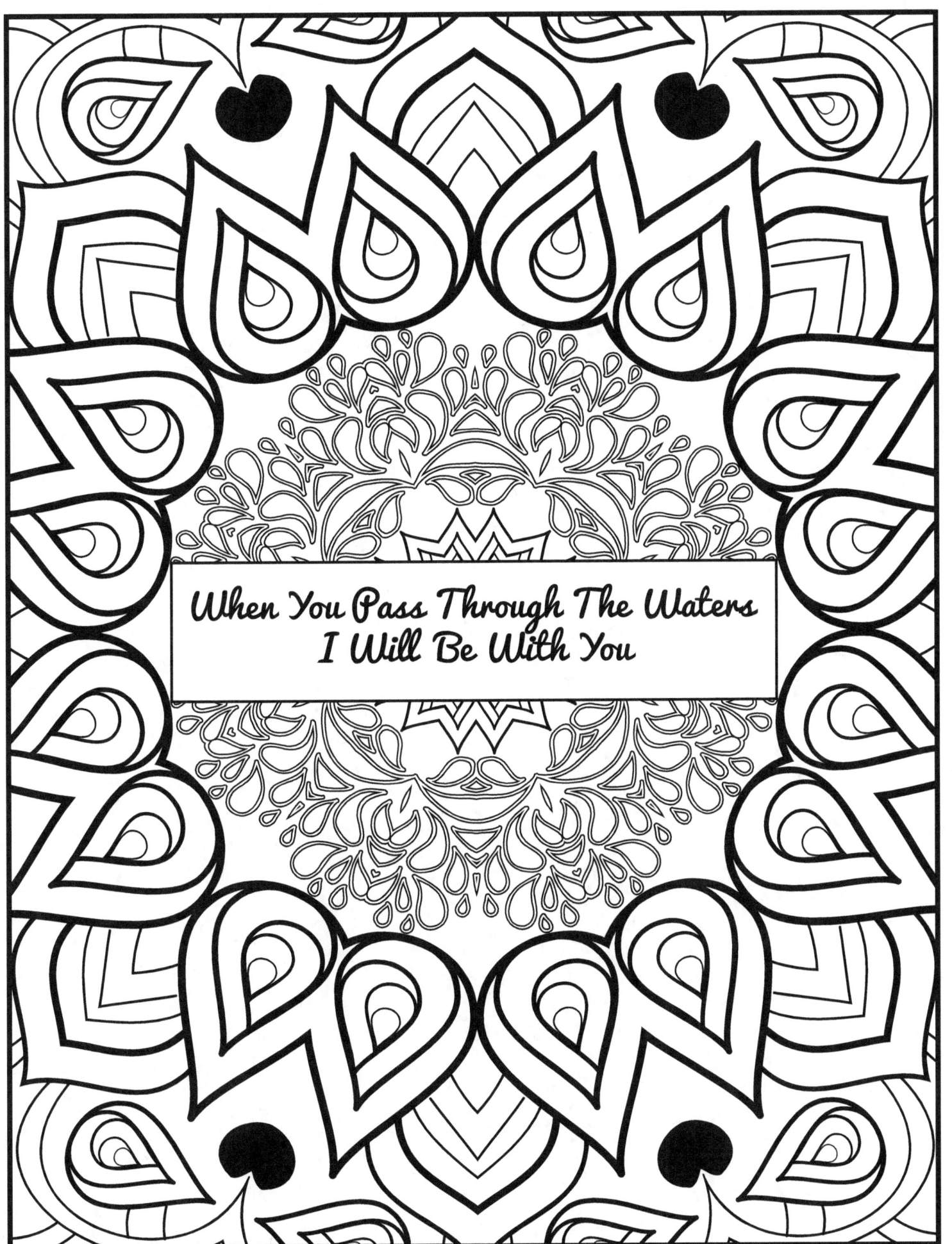

When You Pass Through The Waters
I Will Be With You

Even Though I Walk Through The Darkest Valley,
I Will Fear No Evil

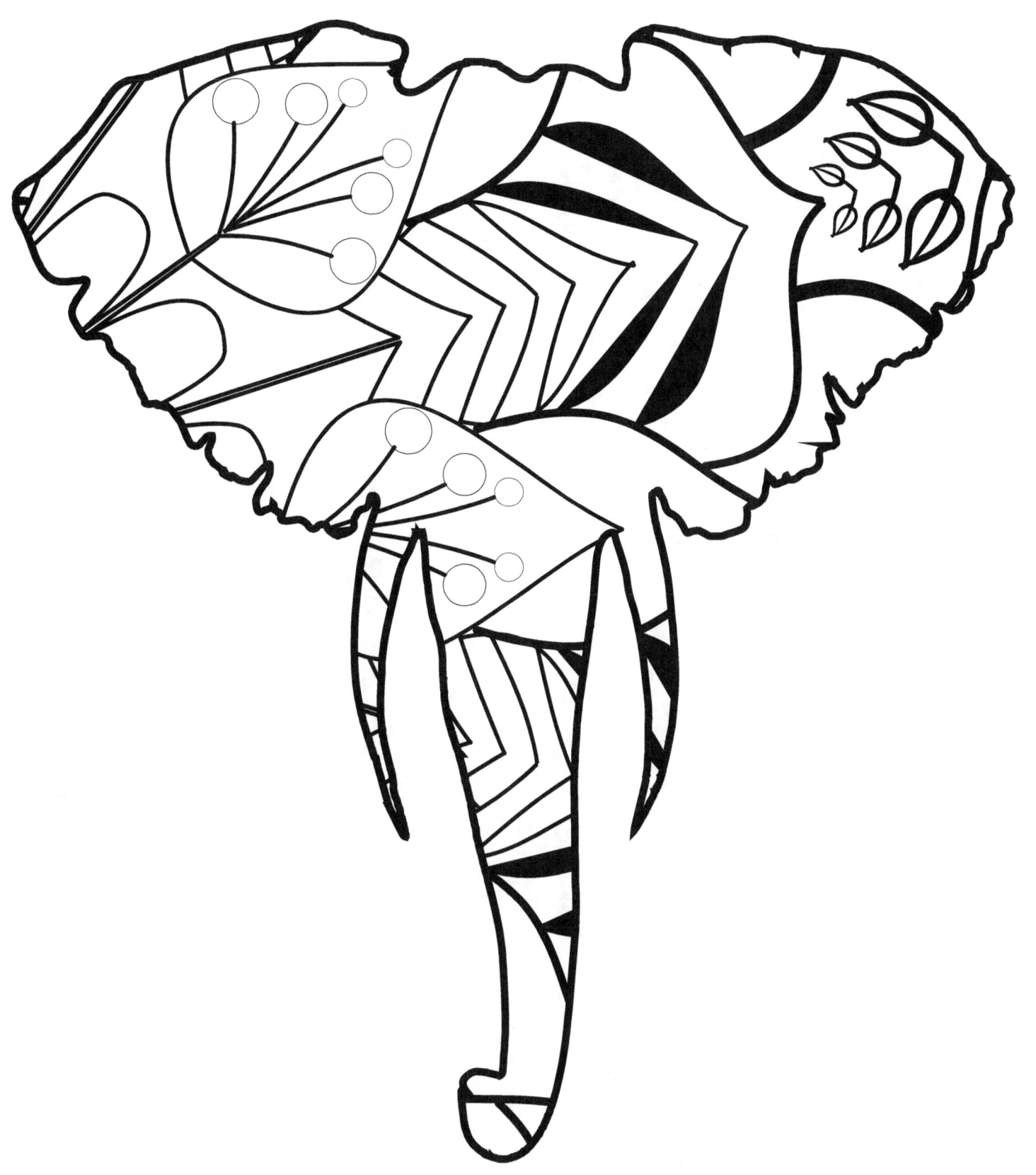

If God Be For You who can Be Against You?

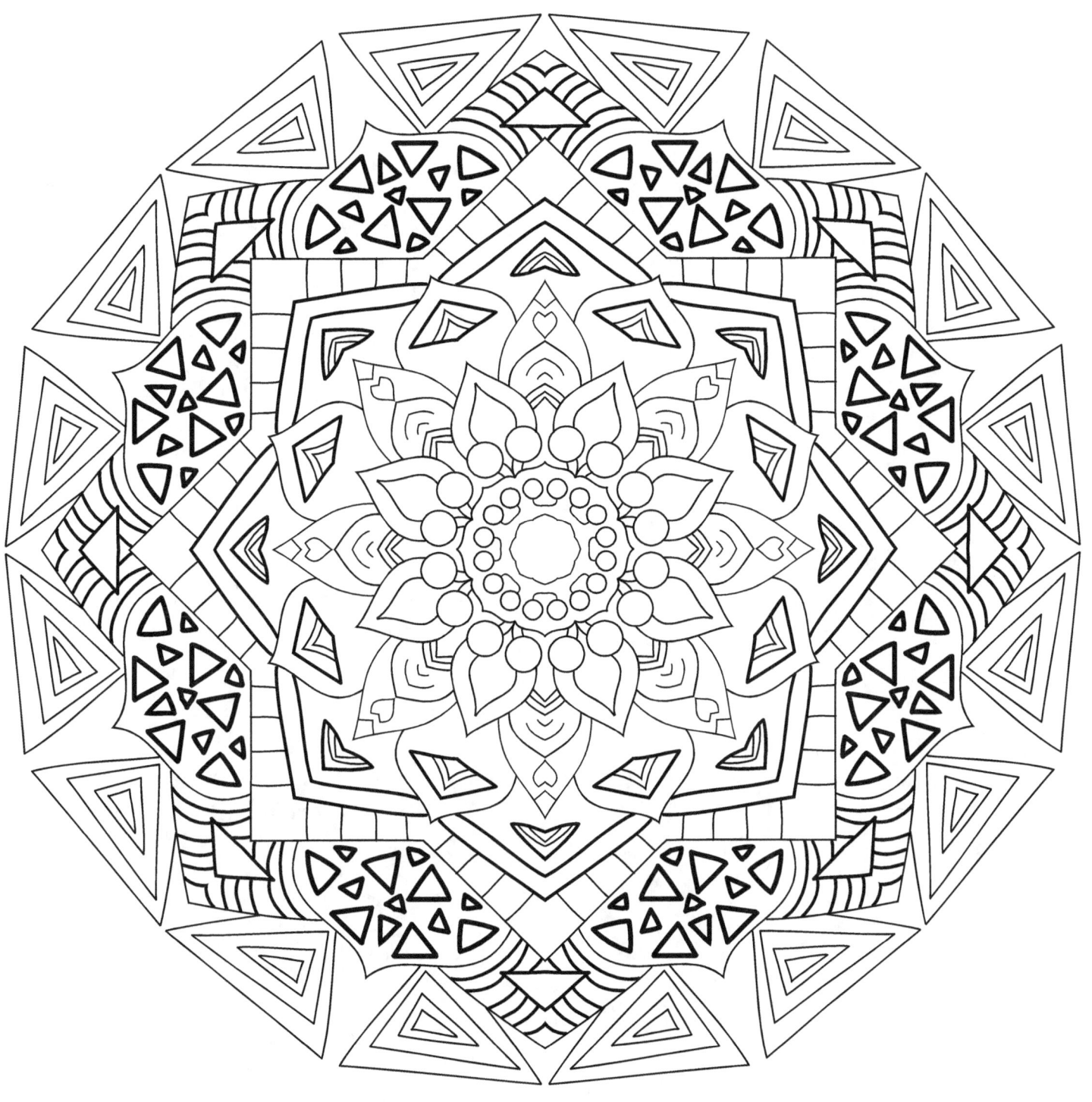

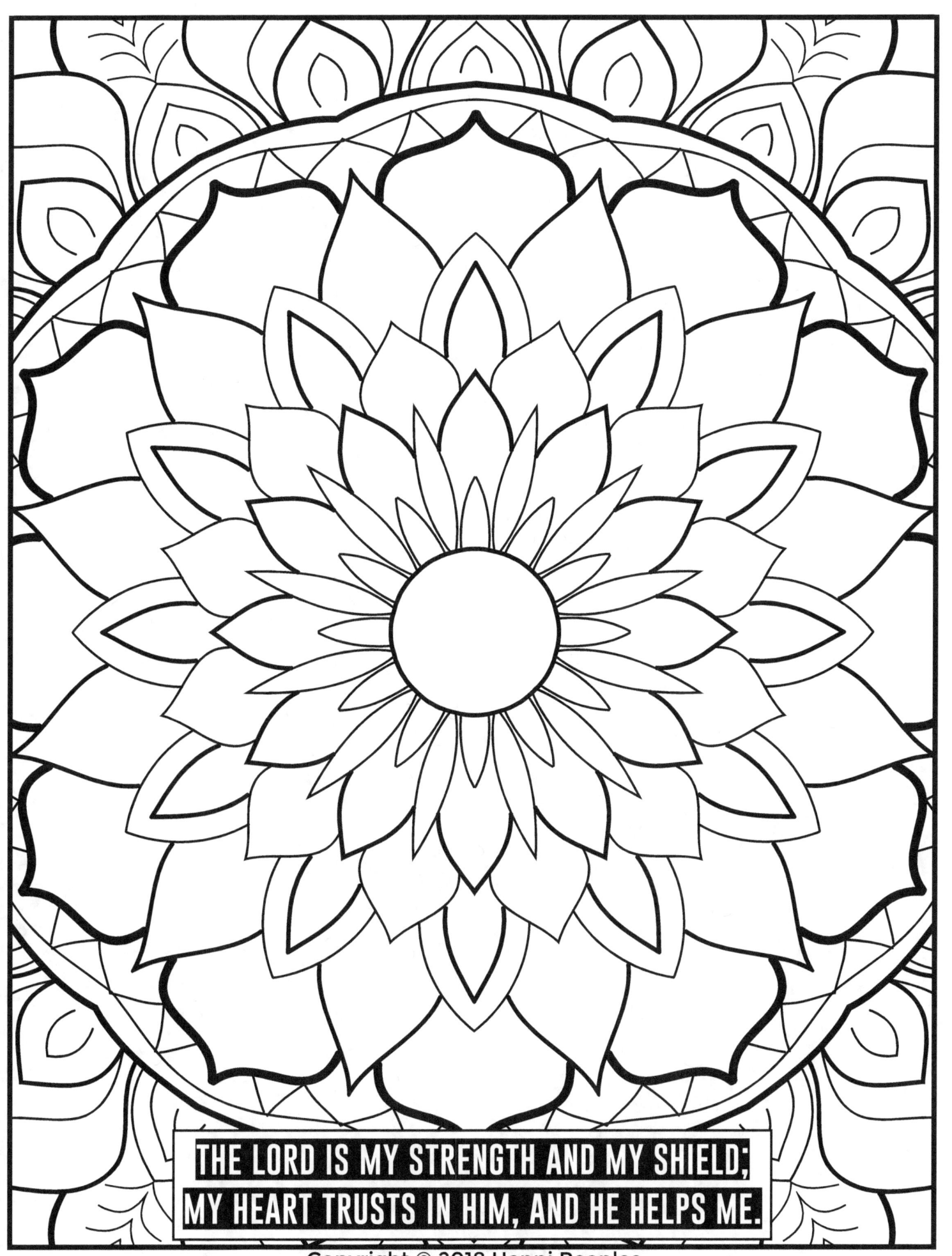

THE LORD IS MY STRENGTH AND MY SHIELD;
MY HEART TRUSTS IN HIM, AND HE HELPS ME.

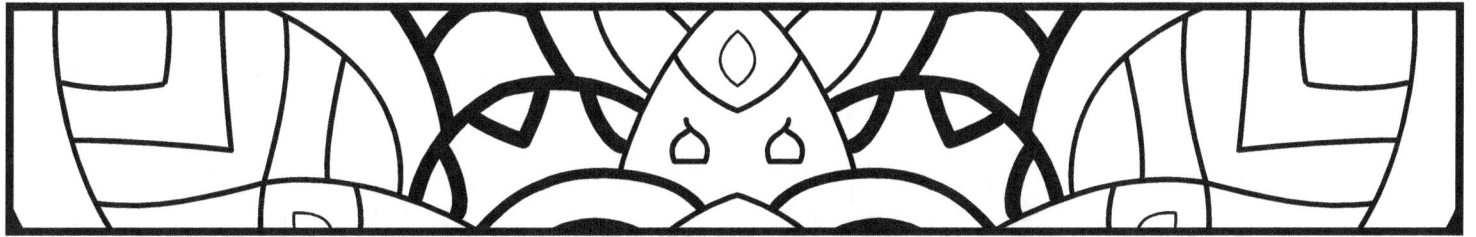

40 Days of Faith Is Available on Amazon.com
Check Out Other Titles In This Series

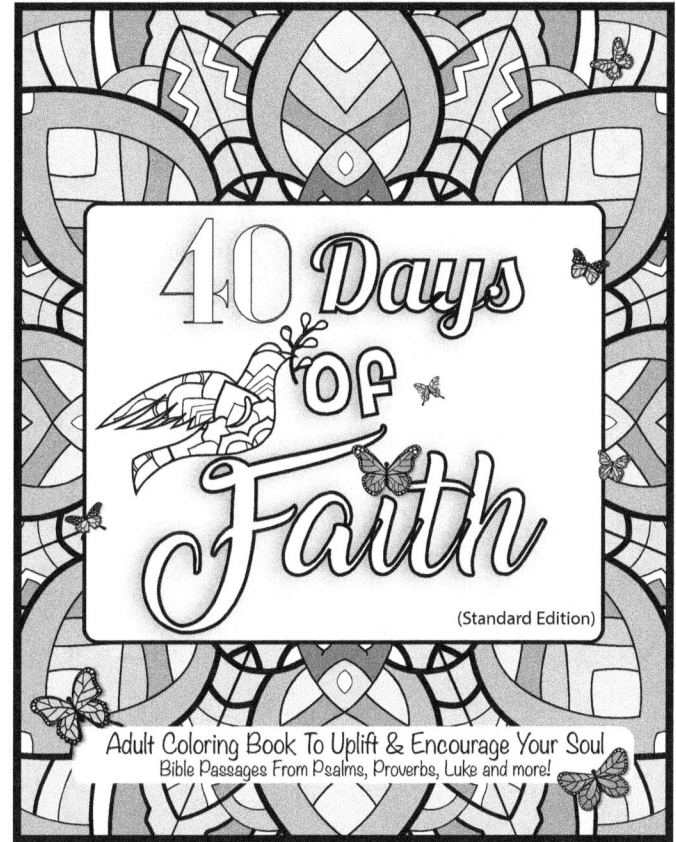

40 Days of Faith (Midnight Edition)
40 Days of Faith (Square Doodle)
40 Days of Faith (Daily Journal)
40 Days of Faith T-Shirts

Available online
For more info visit:
www.Wix.com/HappiPeoples

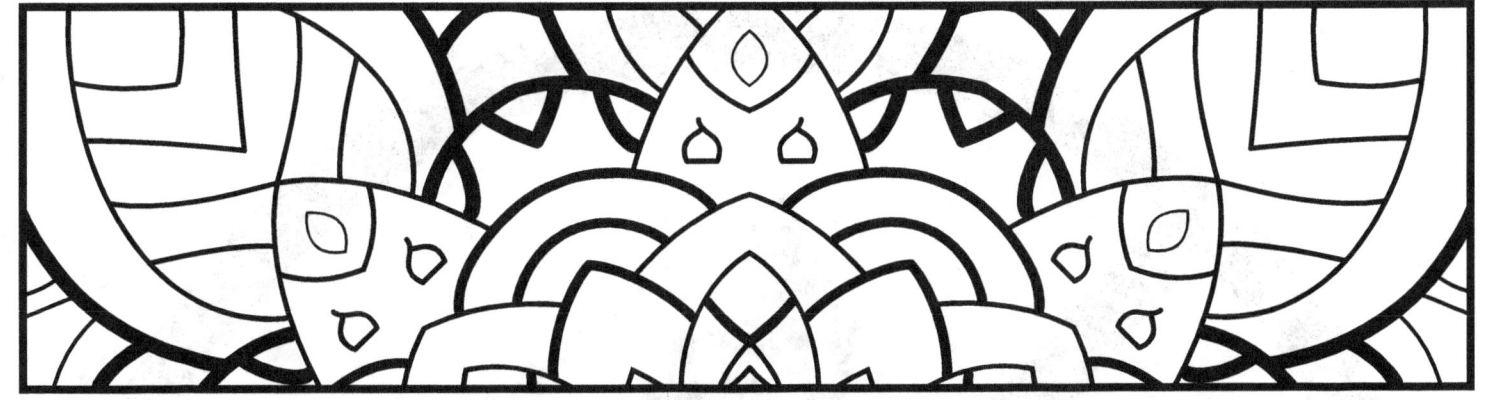

WAIT, BEFORE YOU GO!

Hey There!

I hope you enjoyed coloring,"40 Days of Faith," as much as I've enjoyed creating this book.

You may have noticed your faith getting stronger as you colored these beautiful images, that were inspired by God's Word.

If you haven't already, Join Me Online!
www.Wix.com/HappiPeoples

Share your finshed work with me on Instagram.
www.Instagram.com/HappiPeoples

Share your finshed work with me on Pinterest.
www.pinterest.com/HappiPeoples

Winners are chosen every month to recevie special prizes and give-aways!

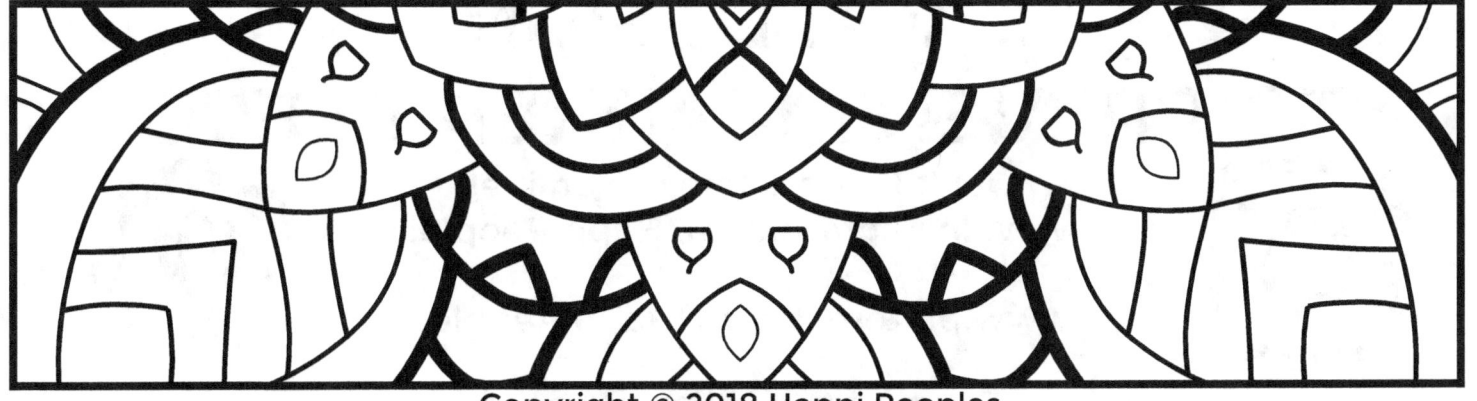

PUT THIS PAGE IN BETWEEN EACH DESIGN
TO PREVENT MARKER BLEED

Don't Forget, Join me online!
www.Instagram.com/HappiPeoples

www.pinterest.com/HappiPeoples

PUT THIS PAGE IN BETWEEN EACH DESIGN TO PREVENT MARKER BLEED

Don't Forget, Join me online!
www.Instagram.com/HappiPeoples

www.pinterest.com/HappiPeoples

www.ingramcontent.com/pod-product-compliance
Lightning Source LLC
Chambersburg PA
CBHW062359220526
45472CB00008B/1870